Gorbachev's Military Policy in the Third World

THE WASHINGTON PAPERS

. . . intended to meet the need for an authoritative, yet prompt, public appraisal of the major developments in world affairs.

President, CSIS: David M. Abshire

Series Editor: Walter Laqueur

Director of Publications: Nancy B. Eddy

Managing Editor: Donna R. Spitler

MANUSCRIPT SUBMISSION

The Washington Papers and Praeger Publishers welcome inquiries concerning manuscript submissions. Please include with your inquiry a curriculum vitae, synopsis, table of contents, and estimated manuscript length. Manuscripts must be between 120–200 double-spaced typed pages. All submissions will be peer reviewed. Submissions to *The Washington Papers* should be sent to *The Washington Papers*; The Center for Strategic and International Studies; 1800 K Street NW; Suite 400; Washington, DC 20006. Book proposals should be sent to Praeger Publishers; One Madison Avenue; New York NY 10010.

The Washington Papers/140

Gorbachev's Military Policy in the Third World

Mark N. Katz

Foreword by William E. Odom

Published with The Center for Strategic and International Studies Washington, D.C.

PRAEGER

New York
Westport, Connecticut
London

Library of Congress Cataloging-in-Publication Data

Katz, Mark N.
    Gorbachev's Military Policy in the Third World
Mark N. Katz.
        p.   cm. – (The Washington papers, ISSN 0278-937X ; 140)
    "Published with the Center for Strategic and International
Studies, Washington, D.C."
        ISBN 0-275-93340-7 (alk. paper). – ISBN 0-275-93341-5 (pbk. :
alk. paper)
        1. Soviet Union – Military policy.   2. Soviet Union – Military
relations – Developing countries.   3. Developing countries – Military
relations – Soviet Union.   4. Soviet Union – Foreign relations – 1975–
    I. Title.   II. Series.
    UA770.K344   1989
    355.033547 – dc20   89-32381

The *Washington Papers* are written under the auspices of The Center
for Strategic and International Studies (CSIS) and published
with CSIS by Praeger Publishers. The views expressed in these papers
are those of the authors and not necessarily those of the Center.

Copyright © 1989 by The Center for Strategic and
International Studies

Library of Congress Catalog Card Number: 89-32381
ISBN: 0-275-93340-7 (cloth)
        0-275-93341-5 (paper)

First published in 1989

Praeger Publishers, One Madison Avenue, New York, NY 10010
A division of Greenwood Press, Inc.

Printed in the United States of America

∞

The paper used in this book complies with the Permanent
Paper Standard issued by the National Information Standards
Organization (Z39.48-1984).

10   9   8   7   6   5   4   3   2   1

To Tain

Contents

Foreword

Mikhail Gorbachev has surprised the West with the degree to which he has been willing to relax East-West tensions in Europe and the Far East. Both scholars and the media keep us apprised daily of the tactics in this new Soviet strategy. This is not surprising, given the direct bearing these events may have on Western security and foreign policy. The East-West competition, however, has never been limited to the advanced industrial world. The intersection of U.S. and Soviet interests and policies in the Third World has also been the locus of much of the competition. By comparison, however, much less media and scholarly attention is devoted to an overall assessment of Soviet Third World policy.

In the past, this imbalance in analytical attention has yielded surprises and gross misestimates of Soviet strategy. The spectacular example is the mid-1970s when East-West détente suffered from Soviet aggressiveness in the Third World. The Soviet transport of Cuban combat troops to Angola in 1975 shocked Secretary of State Henry Kissinger and President Gerald Ford as well as a number of European political leaders. When the Carter administration came to office in 1977, it had not yet understood Leonid Brezhnev's Third World policy. Some of President Jimmy Carter's first initiatives – arms transfer policy, Conventional Arms Control Talks, and the Indian Ocean Arms Talks – rested on the false assumption that the original U.S. image of détente was still viable, even in the Third World. Soviet actions in Ethiopia, South Yemen, Southeast Asia, Central America, and, finally, Afghanistan erased the initial illusions about a muting of Third World competition.

Is the United States making the same mistake today in assessing Soviet strategy? This volume by Mark Katz is an important effort to find the answer. He is especially qualified to investigate the issue because of his earlier study about Soviet military thought on the utility of military power in pursuit of the "international class struggle" in the Third World.

The answer he gives does not wholly justify either Western "hard-liners" or the "soft-liners" in their beliefs that Gorbachev's policies are either a mere ruse under which Third World competition will be stepped up or a genuine strategic withdrawal from the competition. Rather he finds a Soviet tactical retreat to an approach that is less costly. Turning Third World states into reliable Soviet clients has been expensive for Moscow. Gorbachev has apparently concluded that it is essential to cut those costs in some cases and to be cautious about incurring new obligations in the near future. At the same time, Soviet strategy aims to deny U.S. influence and access to contested Third World states and regions.

Gorbachev has introduced a serious ambiguity into official Soviet ideology that complicates our reading of his Third World strategy. He has redefined "peaceful coexistence," a concept originated by Lenin in 1921. Traditionally it has been "a specific form of the international class struggle." It was based on the recognition that a direct military confrontation with the West might lead to Soviet defeat. That required the establishment and maintenance of correct state-to-state relations with the leading capitalist governments. Party-to-party relations were continued in the context of the Communist International. In the colonial regions, however, peaceful coexistence included alliances with anticolonial forces and support of "national liberation movements."

In his 1915 treatise, "Imperialism: The Highest Stage of Capitalism," Lenin defined the colonial system as one organic whole in which capitalist competition for markets and resources had spread into the underdeveloped regions. Although socialist revolutions were not likely to occur there, given the absence or weakness of the local working-class elements, bourgeois nationalist revolutions looked promising. Objectively they would be anti-imperialist. Moreover, because the capitalist system increasingly depended on colonies, these nationalist revolutions might well break the entire capitalist system at its "weakest link." This concept of attacking capitalism in the Third World, of course, has been at the root of Soviet policy ever since, except for the hiatus in World War II.

In his book, *Perestroika*, Gorbachev tells us that "peaceful coexistence" is no longer a "specific form of the international class struggle." "Humankind interests" transcend "class interests" in the nuclear era, and the prevention of war that might involve nuclear weapons is the most pressing "humankind interest." Although this new formulation clearly applies to preventing a major war in Europe, it is not so obvious what it means about wars in the Third World. "Class interests" may be set aside in direct East-West relations, but can they also be subordinated in North-South relations? Gorbachev leaves us uncertain. Many Marxists, if Politburo member Yegor Ligachev is to be believed, are also left uncertain. In the summer of 1988, he told a party audience in Gorki that this idea of "humankind interests" changing the nature of the "international class struggle" was merely confusing people, especially Soviet friends abroad.

Perhaps Gorbachev does not enjoy the kind of broad-based party support that would allow him to be more clear while he draws back from the competition. Or perhaps his ambiguity is intentional because he wants to continue vigorous competition with the United States in the Third World. Both interpretations are logical, and both have been drawn as inferences, but neither has been tested systematically against the available evidence.

Katz's monograph is precisely an effort to assess both Soviet behavior and policy rhetoric. To be sure, he does not give us the last word on the matter. It is much too early for that. He does, however, provide some well-informed first words on the issue, and they suggest an intriguing hypothesis about the rationale of changing Soviet policy. The Cold War is not over in the Third World, but the objective trends, as Katz sees them, are definitely not now in the Soviet Union's favor. Moscow's reaction to the new realities has not been to quit the fight but rather to withdraw selectively for the purpose of strengthening its position in key states while trying to see that the United States does not capitalize on the withdrawals.

Both policymakers and scholars will find this essay stimulating. For policymakers in particular it raises the question of alternative U.S. responses. Should Washington allow the Soviet selective withdrawal and consolidation to go unchallenged? Or should the United States aggressively pursue the Soviet retreat, pressing it further than Gorbachev intends? The former policy could leave Moscow in a stronger position for a new reassertive policy in the Third World 5 or 10 years hence. The latter policy could lead the United States to make the same mistakes that Brezhnev did—overextension and commitment to high-cost clients that are vulnerable to a Soviet counteroffensive.

Students of pro-Soviet movements in the Third World will wonder what their leaders' reactions will be to the new Soviet policy. Can they adjust without losing their own base of support? Will they go their own way, ignoring Soviet policy and seeking other sources of support? Or will they retain their disciplined loyalty to Moscow?

These are only a few of the questions raised by Katz's stimulating essay.

Lt. Gen. William E. Odom, USA (Ret.)
Director of National Security Studies
Hudson Institute

February 1989

About the Author

Mark N. Katz received his Ph.D. in political science from M.I.T. in 1982. He was awarded postdoctoral fellowships by the Rockefeller Foundation and the Woodrow Wilson International Center for Scholars. Katz has held positions at the Brookings Institution, the U.S. Department of State, and the Wilson Center. He has also served as a private consultant. In 1985 he was a visiting scholar at CSIS. Currently an assistant professor of government and politics at George Mason University in Fairfax, Virginia, he will be a fellow at the U.S. Institute of Peace in Washington, D.C. during the 1989–1990 academic year. Katz is the author of *The Third World in Soviet Military Thought* (Johns Hopkins, 1982) and *Russia and Arabia: Soviet Foreign Policy toward the Arabian Peninsula* (Johns Hopkins, 1986), plus several journal and newspaper articles on Soviet relations with the Third World.

Acknowledgments

I thank Francis Fukuyama and Stephen Sestanovich for their comments and suggestions on an earlier draft of this study. I also appreciate the help of my two research assistants, Melissa Dawson and Thomas Firestone.

Summary

This study examines the changes that have occurred in Soviet military policy toward the Third World under Gorbachev. Mikhail Gorbachev has pursued détente with the West more actively than Leonid Brezhnev because the new leader sees this as essential for his ambitious economic reform efforts (perestroika). Although his predecessors also valued détente, Gorbachev understands more clearly than they did that Soviet military involvement in the Third World can weaken it. Because Gorbachev regards détente as so essential for the achievement of perestroika, he has adopted a less aggressive military policy in the Third World in order to pursue détente. Soviet military statements since Gorbachev came to power indicate that the Soviet military, for the most part, does not oppose Gorbachev's retrenchment from the Third World. The Soviet military even seems to approve the decision to withdraw from Afghanistan.

Gorbachev has drastically reduced support to revolutionary groups in the Third World. He also appears far less interested than Brezhnev in acquiring additional military facilities there for the USSR. As the Soviet withdrawal from Afghanistan illustrates, Gorbachev is even willing to give up some allies that previous Soviet leaders thought were important. Soviet statements also indicate that Gorbachev favors the withdrawal of Vietnamese forces from Cambodia even if this means the downfall of the pro-Hanoi regime in Phnom Penh. Nevertheless, Gorbachev does seek to preserve Marxist regimes and Soviet military facilities in Vietnam, South Yemen, and Ethiopia. These bases are important for maintaining the vital sea line of communication between the western and eastern USSR (a function for which Afghanistan and Cambodia are not needed). And although Angola and Nicaragua are less important to the USSR militarily, the cost of preserving Marxist regimes in these countries is far less than in Afghanistan or Cambodia. Gorbachev also seeks to continue Soviet military access to Syria; Syria provides Moscow's only naval base in the Mediterranean.

Yet while Gorbachev has de-emphasized the expansion of Moscow's base network in the Third World, he has vigorously sought to reduce U.S. military access to the Third World. Gorbachev has attempted to do this through a stepped-up diplomatic campaign to convince moderate Third World states that the USSR is not their enemy and hence there is no need to ally with Washington against Moscow. He has also announced or supported regional security proposals for Asia and the Pacific, the Persian Gulf, the Middle East, parts of Africa, Central America, and elsewhere. If the proposals are accepted by the states of these regions, U.S. military access to these states would definitely be reduced. Gorbachev's de-emphasis on obtaining new bases for the USSR could mean that moderate Third World governments may become more amenable to accepting these regional security proposals.

This possibility should be a serious concern for the United States. Nevertheless, Gorbachev faces important obstacles in his efforts to reduce U.S. military access to the Third World. Not least of these is a continuing fear on the part of non-Marxist Third World governments that the USSR could return to a policy of supporting revolution as it has in the past.

Gorbachev's Military Policy in the Third World

Introduction

Soviet foreign and military policy toward the Third World has changed significantly since Mikhail Gorbachev came to power. Most important, Gorbachev has pursued the withdrawal of Soviet troops from Afghanistan despite the strong risk that the Marxist regime in Kabul will be overthrown without this support. The voluntary Soviet withdrawal from Afghanistan is a move that only recently many Western analysts thought would never take place. It represents a highly significant retrenchment in Soviet military commitments and aims in the Third World. Gorbachev also appears to be encouraging Vietnam to withdraw its troops from Cambodia even though this move would risk the return to power of the pro-Chinese Pol Pot forces. In addition, he supports the recent peace settlement for Angola that calls for the withdrawal of Cuban troops.

Yet, while reducing Soviet military commitments in some areas of the Third World, Gorbachev has moved to expand them elsewhere. During 1987, he presided over the largest Soviet naval buildup ever in the Persian Gulf. His vigorous initiatives in various regions also indicate that the Third World continues to be important to Moscow.

Much has already been written about how Gorbachev has reoriented the priorities of Moscow's Third World policy

1

as pursued by Nikita Khrushchev and especially Leonid Brezhnev. Whereas his predecessors emphasized expanding the number of pro-Soviet revolutionary Third World states, Gorbachev has not attempted to do so. Brezhnev in particular regarded revolutionary states, especially Marxist ones, as Moscow's most important allies in the Third World. Gorbachev, on the other hand, has de-emphasized their importance while making greater efforts to improve Soviet relations with the major non-Marxist Third World states.

What do Gorbachev's changing policies toward the Third World indicate about Soviet military objectives there? Has Gorbachev significantly altered the military objectives Moscow pursues in Asia, Africa, and Latin America, or is he pursuing the same ones as his predecessors by different means? To the extent that it can be determined, what is Gorbachev's military policy toward the Third World? It is these questions that this study will examine.

Before proceeding further, however, it is important to note that the term "Soviet military policy" can have at least four different meanings. First, it can refer in a very narrow sense to Soviet military tactics—for example, the battle-field tactics of the Soviet Army in Afghanistan or the configuration of various Soviet flotillas in Third World waters. This definition will not be discussed here.

Second, Soviet military policy can refer in a very broad sense to foreign policy that has a military component—for example, Moscow's sending of arms or military advisers for primarily political goals. Such a policy, although definitely of a military nature, may not significantly affect the military goals of the Soviet Union itself. And because the USSR has military relations to some degree with so many Third World countries, Soviet military policy in this sense is basically equivalent to Soviet foreign policy toward the Third World as a whole. This study will not focus on this broader definition because the subject has already been treated elsewhere. Some discussion of this broader aspect of Soviet military policy toward the Third World, however, is unavoidable.

Third, Soviet military policy can refer to the Soviet military's own policy or policy preferences. This subject, although not the primary focus of the study, will be examined in chapter 2 to determine the extent to which the views of Soviet military leaders and thinkers are in harmony with those of Gorbachev.

Fourth, Soviet military policy can refer to the military objectives sought by Soviet politico-military policy as a whole. The means to secure these military objectives may be either military or nonmilitary. It is this aspect of Soviet military policy that will be analyzed here. Specifically, I will examine how the Gorbachev leadership has defined and pursued Soviet military objectives in the Third World.

Chapter 1 discusses the nature of the military objectives Moscow has pursued in the Third World and the changing domestic and international environment that had led to their reassessment by the Gorbachev leadership. The Soviets have pursued two types of military goals in the Third World: negative ones (such as denying or limiting U.S. access to military facilities) and positive ones (such as acquiring or retaining Soviet access to military facilities). Khrushchev, and especially Brezhnev, pursued positive and negative military goals in the Third World simultaneously. Soviet support for Marxist revolutionaries to come to power somewhere not only would deny the United States military access to this country (a negative goal), but might well give the Soviet Union military access to it (a positive goal).

Gorbachev has de-emphasized the pursuit of positive military objectives in the Third World. Unlike Brezhnev, Gorbachev has placed the highest priority on reforming the Soviet economy. This goal requires that he prevent the Soviet defense budget from rising dramatically, which in turn requires him to restore détente with the United States. Gorbachev cannot hope to keep Soviet defense expenditures down if U.S.-Soviet relations are hostile and U.S. defense expenditures are growing rapidly. Gorbachev has also recognized that détente with the United States can be negatively affected by the spread of Marxist regimes and Soviet military intervention in the Third World. To achieve his higher-priority domestic and foreign policy goals, Gorbachev has de-emphasized the pursuit of positive military goals in the Third World. His willingness to withdraw from Afghanistan indicates that he is not necessarily committed to retaining existing Third World Marxist allies. Nevertheless, Gorbachev's de-emphasis on the pursuit of positive military objectives in the Third World has not led to a reduction in Soviet pursuit of negative military goals there.

Chapter 2 examines the views of Soviet military leaders and thinkers on Gorbachev's retrenchment from the Third World. Even before Gorbachev came to power, Soviet military leaders had become less enthusiastic than in the mid-1970s about military involvement in the Third World. Under Gorbachev, Soviet military writing has paid much less attention to the Third World than it had previously. The writing that has been done on this subject has placed greater emphasis on the difficulties of this type of military involvement as well as on the danger of escalation. The statements of Soviet military leaders also indicate that they do not oppose the withdrawal from Afghanistan. Indeed, the Soviet military seems eager to end its involvement there. Soviet military leaders, however, have been concerned that Soviet armed forces not suffer large casualties during the process of withdrawal and that the military not be blamed for losing the war. For the most part, the Soviet military approves Gorbachev's retrenchment from the Third World and his de-emphasis of the pursuit of positive military goals there.

Chapters 3, 4, and 5 examine how Gorbachev has modified the three primary politico-military means that the Soviets have employed in attempting to achieve their military objectives in the Third World: support for revolution, defense of Third World Marxist allies, and relations with non-Marxist states.

Chapter 3 notes that although the Soviets have achieved a number of positive military objectives through their previous support for revolution in the Third World,

Gorbachev has recognized that there are important costs for Moscow in doing so. Not only can Soviet military support to Marxist revolution negatively affect détente, but several Marxist governments have proven extremely costly for Moscow and its allies to maintain. Even with direct Soviet intervention in Afghanistan, Cuban intervention in Angola, and Vietnamese intervention in Cambodia, the pro-Soviet Marxist regimes in these countries have been unable to defeat their internal opponents. The previous success of Marxist revolution, then, has been a mixed blessing for Moscow. In addition, Gorbachev has come to expect that Marxist revolution is unlikely to be the "wave of the future" in the Third World. For all these reasons, he is unlikely to provide much support for Marxist revolution.

By reducing support for revolution, Gorbachev gives up the potential positive and negative military goals that Moscow might have achieved in countries where revolution succeeded. But as the Soviet withdrawal from Afghanistan shows, Gorbachev is also willing to give up whatever actual positive or negative military goals that the presence of Soviet forces there achieved. Chapter 4 examines how committed Gorbachev is to maintaining Marxist regimes elsewhere in the Third World. Other Marxist Third World regimes serve Moscow's positive military objectives in ways that Afghanistan cannot. Soviet military facilities in Vietnam, South Yemen, and Ethiopia enhance Soviet ability to maintain vital sea lines of communication between the Western USSR and Vladivostok. And Moscow has indicated a strong desire to retain these countries as allies. Gorbachev, then, is not willing to risk the downfall of Marxist regimes that serve vital positive military goals.

Soviet statements do reveal, however, that Moscow would not object to a Vietnamese withdrawal from Cambodia; the Soviet-supported Vietnamese intervention there, as in Afghanistan, has proven extremely costly but unwinnable. In addition, a pro-Soviet Marxist regime in this country does not contribute much to Moscow's positive military goals; what military facilities Moscow needs in this part of the world it already has in Vietnam. Soviet actions and statements about Angola reveal that Gorbachev wants to reduce the heavy cost of propping up the Marxist regime in that country by agreeing to a regional security accord involving a withdrawal of Cuban troops. In contrast to its expectations about Afghanistan and Cambodia, however, Moscow seems to anticipate that the Marxist government will remain in power in Angola and that the USSR will not have to relinquish the military facilities it enjoys there. Finally, although Nicaragua may not be militarily important to the USSR, Gorbachev seems willing to support the Sandinista government's remaining in power: the cost of doing so is not very high, because both the contras and U.S. support for them have proven to be ineffective. The Soviet withdrawal from Afghanistan, then, does not necessarily mean that Gorbachev is willing to accept the downfall of Marxist regimes either in countries that are militarily important to the USSR or even in those that are less militarily important but where the cost of maintaining them in power is relatively modest.

Chapter 5 analyzes how Gorbachev has pursued Soviet military goals with regard to non-Marxist Third World states. In the past, Soviet acquisition of military facilities in Marxist and radical non-Marxist states advanced Moscow's positive military objectives, but hindered the achievement of its negative ones. As the Soviets acquired facilities in various parts of the Third World, neighboring non-Marxist governments often became more fearful of Soviet intentions and sought an increased U.S. military presence in their country or region—a result opposite, of course, to what the Soviets wanted. In addition, some of the non-Marxist states in which Moscow did acquire bases proved unreliable and expelled the Soviet military presence (as occurred in Egypt and Somalia in the mid-1970s).

By de-emphasizing the pursuit of positive military goals, Gorbachev has sought not only to avoid these and other problems, but also to place the USSR in a better position to pursue its negative military goals. Gorbachev has announced regional security proposals for several areas in the Third World, including Asia and the Pacific, the Persian Gulf, the Middle East, the Horn of Africa, and Central America. All of these proposals, if implemented, would serve to limit the expansion of U.S. alliances and military access in these regions. Some would even lead to a reduction of present U.S. military access to these areas. By avoiding actions that non-Marxist states find threatening, Gorbachev seeks to persuade them that the USSR is not their enemy and that there is no need for them to ally with the United States against Moscow. Indeed, he hopes to convince them that it is the United States that threatens their interests and that non-Marxist states can rely upon Soviet help to thwart U.S. aims. This strategy has not yet yielded significant results for the Soviets, but eventually it could.

Chapter 6, the conclusion, notes that Gorbachev's new military policy, if effective, could seriously weaken U.S. military strength in the Third World. Nevertheless, there are several obstacles to successfully implementing this new policy. It will work only if the USSR's behavior is moderate and self-restrained over the long run. Renewed Soviet intervention anywhere could seriously damage Soviet efforts to convince non-Marxist states that the USSR is not a threat to them. Yet even if non-Marxist states eventually consider the USSR less of a threat, they will not necessarily have an interest in reducing or excluding the U.S. military presence in their region. Continued conflict between Third World states ensures that the combatants as well as neighboring states will ask the superpowers for support. If Moscow helps one side, the other will turn to Washington. Even where conflict is not occurring, non-Marxist states may have little incentive to exclude the U.S. military presence from their region. Non-Marxist states might consider improved relations with the USSR as a means to increase their independence vis-à-vis both superpowers; working with Moscow to reduce the U.S. military presence in their regions might retard rather than enhance the achievement of this goal. Thus, even if non-Marxist Third World states come to view the USSR less and less as a threat, Gorbachev faces serious obstacles in attempting to achieve Moscow's negative military goals.

1

The Context of Soviet Military Policy

The military objectives that the Soviet Union has pursued in the Third World can be divided into two broad categories: negative or denial goals and positive or acquisitive goals. Negative Soviet military goals are designed to deny or limit U.S. and allied access to military facilities in the Third World (as well as to the countries and oceans of the Third World generally). The Soviet objective is to limit the ability of the United States and others to act militarily against the interests of the Soviet Union from the Third World. At minimum, the Soviets have sought to prevent the United States and its allies from gaining additional military bases. At maximum, they have sought to deprive the United States and its allies of the access they already possess.

Negative Soviet military goals in the Third World include denying access to military facilities, allies, or the sea to the United States and other countries from which they could more easily (1) launch direct attacks upon the Soviet Union; (2) attack the Soviet Union's allies, including those in the Third World; (3) interdict Soviet sea lines of communication (SLOCs); and (4) strengthen U.S. SLOCs and access to those strategic commodities, such as oil, that would be vital to the United States in the event of an extended

9

conventional conflict between the United States and the USSR.

Positive Soviet military goals are designed to acquire for the Soviet Union and its allies access to military facilities (as well as access to the countries and oceans of the Third World generally). Moscow's objective in seeking these goals is to be able to act against the interests of its primary military rivals. At minimum, the Soviets have sought to retain those military facilities and other positions of strength that they have already acquired. At maximum, they have sought to acquire additional facilities, allies, and military access.

Positive Soviet military goals include the acquisition of access to military facilities, allies, or the sea so that the USSR and its allies could more easily (1) attack military assets of the United States and its allies in the event of a general U.S.-Soviet conflict; (2) militarily intervene to support Moscow's various Third World allies; (3) secure Soviet SLOCs; (4) interdict Western SLOCs and access to strategic commodities during a protracted conventional conflict with the United States; and (5) induce U.S. military planners to deploy forces and plan contingencies in areas of great U.S., but small Soviet, concern to distract them from areas of greater Soviet concern.

That these have been Moscow's precise military goals, of course, is not exactly clear. The Soviets have not forthrightly stated what their military goals — particularly in the positive sense — are in the Third World. Some of these goals can be inferred from Soviet statements: the Soviets have repeatedly denounced the U.S. military presence in Third World countries and waters, claiming that it is a threat to all nations, including the USSR. Other goals can be inferred from Soviet military actions: Moscow has in the past used bases in the Third World to facilitate its own or allied military intervention there. Still others are only logical: because the Soviet Navy maintains a significant presence in the Third World, it is only prudent for Western military planners to assume that Moscow would attempt to defend Soviet SLOCs and interdict Western ones in time of conflict. Finally, Western analysts have feared that the Soviets have such long-term military goals as denying the West access to Persian Gulf oil or strategic minerals in southern Africa. The evidence as to whether this is or ever has been their intention is ambiguous.

It is important to note that positive and negative military objectives are quite distinct from each other: the goal of the former is to strengthen the power of the Soviet Union while the goal of the latter is to weaken the power of Moscow's adversaries, particularly the United States.

The Soviets, of course, have pursued objectives other than military ones in the Third World. In the past, Moscow has encouraged Marxist revolutions or coups in many Third World countries (for example, Benin) that have little strategic significance. The goal of increasing the number of Marxist states itself was considered a valuable political aim. The West would be denied an alliance with such a country, and the Soviets could make some military use of it, although such use might only be of secondary importance. In addition, the Soviets have pursued good relations with many Third World states—even ones closely allied with the United States—to fulfill their political, ideological, diplomatic, or economic objectives with little expectation of furthering any specific military objectives. Before Gorbachev came to power, Soviet leaders saw the pursuit of both military and nonmilitary objectives in the Third World as complementary.

Various Soviet leaders have placed different emphases on pursuing positive and negative Soviet military objectives in the Third World. During the interwar years, Soviet leaders placed much greater emphasis on the negative goal of weakening Western military access to the colonial world than on the positive goal of increasing Soviet military access to it. During the 1920s, Leon Trotsky advocated Soviet support for revolution in the colonies with the expectation that such support would exacerbate internal contradictions between the bourgeoisie and the proletariat in the European colonial powers and thus lead to revolution in them. Stalin did not share Trotsky's optimism, but at various times he did promote revolution in the Third World to weaken the ability of such colonial powers as Britain and France to act against Soviet interests. When he wanted to ally with Britain and France against Germany, however, he quickly halted Communist revolutionary activity in British and French colonies. No real effort was made to pursue positive military objectives: the Soviets did not then have the means to acquire and defend military access to the Third World. This was a period when the Western powers dominated the Third World, the USSR had little influence in it, and the Soviet state was relatively weak as well as preoccupied with security concerns in Europe and the Far East.[1]

Khrushchev pursued Soviet military policy toward the Third World under very different circumstances than Stalin did. On the one hand, the Third World offered greater opportunities for the Soviets: the European colonial powers were retreating from Asia and Africa. And in several countries radical leaders came to power who were anti-Western, pro-Soviet, and enamoured of the socialist model of development. Furthermore, the USSR had acquired a much increased (though still limited) ability to extend its armed forces into the Third World, at least in peacetime. On the other hand, the United States was threatening Soviet interests from several positions in or near the Third World: Polaris nuclear-powered ballistic missile submarines (SSBNs) could strike targets in the USSR from the Mediterranean, and the formation of the South East Asia Treaty Organization (SEATO) and the Central Treaty Organization (CENTO) threatened the USSR's allies and the USSR itself.

Unlike Stalin, whose military aims in the Third World were relatively vague, Khrushchev had highly specific military objectives there. He wanted to obtain naval facilities in the Mediterranean to enhance Soviet antisubmarine warfare (ASW) capability against U.S. Polarises. He attempted to obtain such facilities in Egypt beginning in the mid-

1950s. After losing base rights in Albania in 1961, obtaining naval facilities in Egypt became even more crucial to Soviet military objectives.[2] Khrushchev also sought to break up CENTO and to seek allies against it; alliance with Egypt and later with Iraq were crucial in this effort. He saw the coming to power of a Marxist regime in Cuba as an opportunity to deploy Soviet intermediate-range ballistic missiles (IRBMs) and medium-range ballistic missiles (MRBMs), thereby counterbalancing U.S. deployment of nuclear forward-based systems in Western Europe and Turkey. Although he did not succeed in maintaining Soviet missiles in Cuba, he did succeed in inducing Washington to remove its missiles from Turkey and to pledge not to invade Cuba — which later proved very useful in helping the Soviets achieve other military objectives.[3]

Whereas Stalin did not pursue positive military goals in the Third World, Khrushchev pursued both positive and negative ones simultaneously. Not only did he want to deny the United States and the West military access to several Third World countries, he also sought to ally them militarily with the USSR where possible. Nevertheless, Khrushchev pursued his negative military goals in the Third World more vigorously and more generally than his positive ones. This was an era when the United States still enjoyed nuclear and conventional military superiority over the Soviet Union and when the United States appeared willing to actively defend its interests in the Third World by military means.

Although his actions in the Third World were hardly timid, Khrushchev was afraid that a U.S.-Soviet military clash there could escalate into a world war. Fearful of the consequences that a world war would have for the USSR when the United States was militarily stronger, Khrushchev valued peaceful coexistence with the West more highly than aid to national liberation movements.[4]

The overall political and military environment in which Moscow pursued military objectives in the Third World was different for Brezhnev than it was for Khrushchev, especially in the 1970s. During the late 1960s, U.S. involvement in the Vietnam war became increasingly unpopular with the U.S. public. By the time the United States withdrew its forces from Indochina in 1973, the U.S. public was clearly unlikely to tolerate future U.S. involvement in Third World counterinsurgency operations. Just at this point, however, the balance of strength between Marxist guerrillas and European colonial powers or pro-Western regimes moved in favor of the guerrillas in several countries. Furthermore, the Soviets achieved strategic parity with the United States during this period. To Moscow, it appeared that the U.S. government was more desperate for strategic arms control agreements than the USSR was. Despite U.S. complaints of increased Soviet military involvement in the Third World, the Soviets saw that Washington pursued SALT talks with Moscow despite this activity – until, of course, the Soviets intervened in Afghanistan.[5]

Yet in addition to facing a more permissive environment, the Brezhnev leadership saw important reasons for actively pursuing military objectives in the Third World. The Brezhnev leadership understood more fully than Khrushchev that China was likely to remain a permanent opponent. Besides dramatically increasing Soviet troop strength on the Sino-Soviet border, the Soviets took measures to establish a secure SLOC between the western USSR and Vladivostok. This was important because land lines of communication between the western USSR and Siberia were extremely limited. Indeed, the only land link was the Trans-Siberian Railway, which ran perilously close to the Chinese border in some places, and later the more northerly Baikal-Amur Magistral. The possibility that the Chinese could seize or disrupt Soviet train lines made securing the sea link a vital military objective. Such action entailed pursuing the positive goal of securing reliable naval facilities for the Soviet Union along the long sea routes that ran through Third World waters between the western and eastern USSR.

There were other goals as well. Michael MccGwire's research concluded that in the mid-1960s, Soviet military planners began to prepare for the possibility of a long conventional war with the United States instead of a short but devastating nuclear one. His conclusion, if true, suggests that the Soviets would have wanted an increased capability to interdict U.S. SLOCs, some of which also run through Third World waters, as well as to protect Soviet ones. The Soviets developed military objectives in the Third World even in the event of a nuclear war with the United States: as U.S. submarine-launched ballistic missiles (SLBMs) and the SSBNs carrying them both increased their ranges, U.S. SLBMs targeted on the USSR could be fired from waters at a much greater distance from the Soviet Union. What this meant was that the ability to mount ASW efforts against U.S. SSBNs in the Mediterranean became less important as the Polaris was withdrawn from service, but the ability to conduct ASW farther afield—in the Indian Ocean, for example—became more so.[6]

As a result of the many Marxist and non-Marxist states that became allied to the Soviet Union during the Brezhnev era, the Soviet military gained access to additional countries, which enhanced its ability to pursue both positive and negative military goals. Many of these allies, however, were involved in conflict with powerful internal or external opponents. The Soviets had two important objectives in assisting to a greater or lesser extent in the defense of these regimes: the political goal of preventing a Marxist regime from being overthrown and the positive military goal of retaining the military facilities the USSR enjoyed in these countries. The defense of Marxist and other allied regimes was not a mission that the Soviets had either the necessity or the ability to undertake to as great an extent before the Brezhnev era. It was a mission, however, that the Brezhnev leadership found important enough to undertake energetically.

The interregnum years of general secretaries Yuri Andropov and Konstantin Chernenko did not witness much change in the importance of Soviet military objectives in the Third World to overall Soviet external and internal policy. Although Andropov in particular may have been less enthusiastic about military involvement in the Third World, he did not appreciably alter Brezhnev's Third World policies during his brief tenure.[7] This was true despite the fact that since the Soviet invasion of Afghanistan, Soviet military involvement in the Third World had halted progress on arms control and denied the Soviets the assurance of stability in the nuclear arms race they had hoped to achieve through the Senate ratification of the 1979 SALT II accords.

By the time Gorbachev came to power in 1985, the environment in which the USSR pursued its military objectives in the Third World had changed dramatically. Unlike Brezhnev, Gorbachev had ambitious plans to reform and modernize the Soviet economy. These plans have been discussed in great detail elsewhere. What is important to note here is Gorbachev's apparent conclusion that if there is a continuation of economic stagnation in the USSR and dynamic economic growth in the West, the USSR might lose the relative economic strength needed to remain a true superpower in the next century. The only way to obtain the needed resources to foster economic growth was to hold down and preferably reduce such economically unproductive expenditures as defense. To limit the size of the Soviet defense budget, however, Gorbachev needed to establish détente with the West. He wanted to avoid a high-technology arms race that would absorb resources needed for perestroika while not necessarily increasing the security of the Soviet Union as long as it continued.

During the 1970s Brezhnev did not have domestic goals upon which his military policy in the Third World impinged. Nor did Soviet involvement in the Third World appear to affect the pursuit of arms control with the United States any more than temporarily slowing it down at times. Brezhnev, then, apparently did not perceive any serious negative effects from his vigorous pursuit of positive and negative military goals in the Third World. For Gorbachev, however, the domestic goal of reforming the Soviet economy had the highest priority. Because this could only come about through détente with the West, détente also became a high priority. The Gorbachev leadership clearly recognized that aggressive Soviet military involvement in the Third World hurt the prospects for détente and for the success of perestroika. The relationship between an aggressive Soviet military policy toward the Third World and poor prospects for achieving both détente and perestroika was explicitly acknowledged in a May 1988 *Literaturnaya Gazeta* article by a Soviet historian:

> Could such a severe exacerbation of tension in Soviet-Western relations in the late seventies and early eighties have been avoided? Unquestionably so. It is our conviction that the crisis was caused chiefly by the miscalculations and incompetent approach of the Brezhnev leadership toward the resolution of foreign policy tasks.
>
> Though we were politically, militarily (via weapons supplies and advisers), and diplomatically involved in regional conflicts, we disregarded their influence on the relaxation of tension between the USSR and the West and on their entire system of relationships. There were no clear ideas of the Soviet Union's true national state interests. These interests lay by no means in chasing petty and essentially formal gains associated with leadership coups in certain developing countries. The genuine interest lay in ensuring a favorable international situation for profound transformations in the Soviet Union's economy and sociopolitical system. However, at that time it was believed that no transformations were needed. . . . [8]

Acting upon these conclusions, Gorbachev has moved to reduce or eliminate several Soviet military activities in the Third World that are costly both in budgetary outlays and relations with the West. As is now well known, Gorbachev has undertaken the withdrawal of Soviet troops from

Afghanistan. The war there had become a seemingly endless drain on Soviet resources with little prospect of defeating the opposition. Soviet involvement in Afghanistan had also damaged Soviet relations with the West and much of the Third World. Similarly, Gorbachev has encouraged a withdrawal of Vietnamese forces from Cambodia that has now apparently begun in earnest. That conflict, underwritten by the Soviets, had also become expensive, and Moscow's Vietnamese allies also had little prospect of defeating the opposition. Its fruitless continuation only hurt Gorbachev's efforts to improve Soviet relations with China and the countries belonging to the Association of South East Asian Nations (ASEAN).

Moscow has also encouraged a peaceful resolution of the conflict in Angola involving the withdrawal of Cuban troops from Angola as well as South African troops from both that country and Namibia. Previously, the Soviets had called for the withdrawal of South African troops from Namibia and resisted U.S. efforts to link this to a Cuban withdrawal from Angola.[9] To a greater or lesser degree in each case, Gorbachev's policy risks the downfall of a pro-Soviet Marxist government in all three countries – a prospect that Brezhnev was willing to expend considerable resources to avoid.

Gorbachev had also de-emphasized Soviet support for revolution in the Third World – a policy that, although never expensive to pursue in budgetary terms, often led to costly efforts to maintain the Marxists in power once power was achieved. It also negatively affected détente with the United States and the West.[10] Finally, Gorbachev has drastically reduced Soviet naval presence throughout the world. Soviet naval activity grew considerably over two decades to a peak in 1984, but has declined steadily since Gorbachev came to power.[11] This reduction in Soviet naval activity could be intended not only to save money, but also to project a more benign image of the Soviet Union to the West and the Third World.

These changes that Gorbachev has made in Soviet military policy toward the Third World indicate that he places much less value on the positive military goals that Brezhnev pursued in the Third World. By not actively aiding revolution in the Third World, he shows that he does not believe the USSR needs additional military allies there – at least, not ones as likely to remain as loyal to Moscow as pro-Soviet Marxist ones have (and as non-Marxist ones have not). Indeed, it is obvious that Gorbachev does not think that the USSR's Marxist allies in Afghanistan and Cambodia are worth paying too high a price to defend. Gorbachev also clearly values less than Brezhnev whatever military or political objectives that Brezhnev thought they served. Reduced Soviet naval deployments in the Third World could mean that Gorbachev has less interest in such positive military objectives as better enabling the Soviets to attack U.S. military targets and Western SLOCs or to intervene forcefully in the Third World. Whether Gorbachev actually has these goals, however, is less clear: while Soviet naval activities have declined, Soviet shipbuilding plans have not.[12]

It may appear that Gorbachev is also less committed to pursuing negative military goals in the Third World. After all, a decreased deployment of Soviet forces in Third World waters means that Moscow is less able to deny its opponents access to the sea from which they could launch attacks on the USSR, attack Soviet allies, or interdict Soviet SLOCs. Decreased Soviet aid to revolution also means that Gorbachev is not seeking to deprive the West of Third World allies through the traditional Soviet method of working to subvert pro-Western governments.

But although Gorbachev has de-emphasized the pursuit of positive military goals in the Third World, he has not reduced Soviet commitment to achieving negative or denial goals there. Gorbachev's efforts to improve relations with the major non-Marxist Third World states are unlikely to result in their becoming the firm Soviet allies the Marxist regimes are. Nor does Gorbachev seek this. What he does seek, however, is to eliminate fear of the Soviet Union as an incentive for these important non-Marxist states to ally with the United States. He intends not only to prevent them from further increasing their military relations with the United States, but also to diminish the military ties that already exist.

Gorbachev's predecessors, of course, also attempted to achieve negative military objectives by allying with non-Marxist states and advancing peace proposals. The primary difference between Gorbachev's pursuit of these negative military goals and his predecessors' is that Gorbachev has decoupled them from the simultaneous pursuit of positive military goals. This point is significant because Gorbachev's decreased emphasis on positive military goals may increase Soviet opportunities to achieve negative military ones.

It would be ironic indeed if Gorbachev succeeds in reducing the U.S. military presence in the Third World by making a virtue of the decreased Soviet military presence that he considers necessary for other reasons. It is possible that by de-emphasizing positive military goals and pursuing negative ones more assiduously, Gorbachev's military policy toward the Third World may threaten U.S. interests more than Brezhnev's ham-fisted policy, which pursued positive and negative objectives simultaneously.

Nevertheless, although Gorbachev has de-emphasized the pursuit of positive military goals, he has not necessarily abandoned them altogether. Nor does the de-emphasis of positive military goals necessarily mean that there are no obstacles to his achievement of negative ones. At a time when Gorbachev's authority is far from secure, one such obstacle could be the desire of powerful groups, especially the military, to renew the vigorous pursuit of positive military goals in the Third World. The Soviet military's preferences regarding military policy in the Third World will be examined in the next chapter.

2

The Soviet Military's View of Gorbachev's Third World Policy

Does the Soviet military approve or disapprove of Gorbachev's retrenchment from the Third World? Has he presided over the Soviet withdrawal from Afghanistan with the military's concurrence or despite its opposition? Does the Soviet military leadership object to Gorbachev's de-emphasis of positive military goals in the Third World?

The answers to these questions have important implications for the future. If the Soviet military leadership strongly objects to Gorbachev's reduced military activity in the Third World, it is likely to advocate a much more aggressive and activist military policy should Gorbachev become weaker politically or be overthrown altogether. But if the Soviet military leadership has become generally wary of an activist military policy in the Third World, it is likely to advocate a cautious military policy no matter who is in power.

This chapter will examine Soviet military statements under Gorbachev to determine the Soviet military's preferences for policy toward the Third World. Special attention will be paid to the Soviet military's reaction to the withdrawal from Afghanistan. Soviet military thinking about the Third World since the 1970s will be reviewed first to provide a basis for judging how it has evolved under Gorbachev.

Before Gorbachev

During the 1970s, Soviet military writers were rather optimistic about the prospects for achieving Soviet military goals in the Third World with minimum complications. This optimism was expressed through discussions about the possibility that local war in the Third World could escalate to world war between the United States and the USSR. During the 1950s and 1960s, Soviet military writers frequently warned that such escalation could occur. As late as 1968, one such writer noted, "The danger of local wars to peace lies in their possible escalation to a world war, if the nuclear powers are drawn into the conflict."[13]

By the 1970s, however, Soviet military thinkers declared that the USSR had become so strong that it could prevent local war from escalating. The possibility that local war could turn into world war still existed, but was not inevitable. One noted Soviet military thinker pointed out that "with the change in the balance of forces in the international arena in favor of socialism, another possibility is also increasing more and more — that of preventing the development of local wars into an enormous clash on a world-wide scale."[14] This statement reflected the growing confidence of the Brezhnev years that the USSR and its allies could successfully intervene in the Third World.

Also during the early 1970s, the top Soviet military leadership advocated the pursuit of a "liberating mission." This mission entailed active Soviet military assistance both to national liberation movements and to "progressive" (that is, pro-Soviet) regimes. Admiral Sergei Gorshkov, commander-in-chief of the Soviet Navy, was a particularly strong advocate of this mission. He saw it as a way to enhance the role of the navy as well as enlarge its size. The defense minister, Marshal Andrei Grechko, and the chief of the Main Political Administration, General A. A. Yepishev, were also advocates of the liberating mission.[15]

Finally, the Third World was a prominent subject in Soviet military writing during these years. This literature was generally optimistic about the diminution of U.S. influence in Asia, Africa, and Latin America as "progressive" forces gained strength, with the help of the USSR.[16]

Even in the late 1970s, however, Soviet military writing displayed some signs of declining enthusiasm for increased military involvement in the Third World. Francis Fukuyama has pointed out that advocacy of the liberating mission by the top Soviet military leadership declined markedly after the death of Grechko in 1976. The ideas of Admiral Gorshkov were downgraded, as was the role of the navy generally. This may well have occurred because the Soviet General Staff, dominated by the army, did not want to allow the navy to gain a more prominent, independent role than it had or to hurt the interests of the other services by gaining an increased share of the defense budget for expensive new ships.[17]

The military writers who specialized in the Third World remained optimistic about Soviet prospects in this region, although they generally recognized that the achievement of Soviet goals was not necessarily easy. Renewed attention was given to studying the counterinsurgency efforts of the United States and the West in the Third World. Although these Western efforts were characterized as unsuccessful or "doomed to failure" in the 1960s and 1970s, in the early 1980s they were seen to have effective elements.[18] Attention was also paid to the successful Soviet counterinsurgency efforts against Moslem Central Asian rebels (the "Basmachi") in the 1920s and 1930s; this experience was explicitly said to have applications to Soviet involvement in Afghanistan.[19] In the early 1980s before Gorbachev came to power, Soviet military experts appeared to conclude that the USSR and its allies could win against insurgents in ongoing wars, although the top leadership did not want to undertake any more such commitments.

The Gorbachev Years

Since Gorbachev came to power, the Third World has become a less prominent subject in Soviet military thought. A volume edited by B. V. Panov, *Istoriya voennogo iskusstva*, was published the year before Gorbachev came to power and contained an entire section on local wars. This discussion paralleled the detailed treatment of local wars in the Third World published in 1981 by General of the Army I. Shavrov, then chief of the General Staff Academy. Although Panov noted the danger that local war could escalate to world war, he also asserted that it could be increasingly prevented because of the growing "economic and military might of the countries of the socialist camp."[20] This statement was similar to previous optimistic Soviet military assessments of the relationship between local war and world war, implying that Soviet involvement in the Third World did not risk conflict with the United States.

Yet by 1986, only two years later, a collective volume also entitled *Istoriya voennogo iskusstva* (this time edited by P. A. Zhilin) contained no section on local wars in the Third World.[21] Soviet military writers returned to the earlier line of the 1950s and 1960s, emphasizing the risk that local war could escalate into world war. One such statement published by *Kommunist Vooruzhennykh Sil* in April 1987 deserves quotation:

> The peculiarities of world development and of the modern revolutionary process demand at the same time the submission of certain changes in the strategy and tactics of the revolutionary struggle, and stipulate the need for new political thinking. . . . The nuclear era demands the utmost forethought from the revolutionary forces in making decisions on the forms of struggle. The problems of choosing the correct forms of this struggle are currently growing into a problem for the very existence of mankind. . . .
>
> Now there truly exists a great danger of interna-

tionalizing internal conflicts. Due to the interference of imperialist counterrevolutionary forces, a liberation war can grow into a regional conflict. And this does not rule out a sharp deterioration in the international situation as a whole, and a heightened threat of world war.[22]

This more pessimistic view of the relationship between local war and world war may reflect disillusionment with the elusiveness of victory for the USSR and its allies in defending Third World Marxist regimes as well as a genuine fear of a superpower clash as a result of the Reagan administration's more active military involvement in the Third World.[23] Whatever its cause, this trend supports Gorbachev's own preference for a reduced emphasis on Soviet involvement in Third World conflict and an increased effort to promote peaceful coexistence.

Especially since the signing of the Intermediate-Range Nuclear Force (INF) agreement, prospects for U.S.-Soviet détente have increased, and prospects for superpower conflict have decreased. Does this mean that the Soviet military will be more willing to become involved in Third World conflicts? Increased Soviet military involvement occurred with the onset of détente in the 1970s. It is not clear whether the Soviet military sees the possibility of escalation from local war to world war as less likely since 1988; there is no strong indication that it does. The foreign policy leadership in the party, however, definitely does not see renewed détente as an opportunity for increased military involvement in the Third World. Instead, it recognizes that such involvement can harm détente. In an article published in October 1988, a high-level Soviet Foreign Ministry official wrote, "Our direct and indirect involvement in regional conflicts lead to colossal losses by increasing general international tension, justifying the arms race, and hindering the establishment of mutually advantageous ties with the West."[24]

Afghanistan

Statements by Soviet military leaders indicate that they do not oppose the decision to end the Soviet military commitment to defend the Marxist regime in Afghanistan. Several high-ranking military officials have endorsed this decision.[25] Along with the civilian press, the military press has published articles portraying the hopelessness of the fight and expressing approval of the decision to withdraw.[26]

One issue that the Soviet military does appear to be concerned about, however, is that it not be blamed for the failure to secure the Kabul regime in power. The military newspaper *Krasnaya Zvezda* and the Soviet media generally have published numerous statements insisting that the withdrawal is by no means a defeat.[27] Another issue that the Soviet military is extremely concerned about is the safety of the "limited contingent" as it leaves the country. Several statements have been issued threatening quite bluntly that attacks upon withdrawing Soviet troops would be "crushed." According to the commander of Soviet forces in Afghanistan, "Retribution would immediately follow any attempt to disrupt the [withdrawal] schedule."[28] The specific nature of the promised retaliation under these circumstances indicated that the Soviet military intended to carry out this threat.

Soviet military leaders have indicated that Soviet advisers could remain in Afghanistan after the troop pullout. They are not firmly committed, however, to maintaining advisers there after the withdrawal. When asked if this would occur, General A. D. Lizichev (chief of the Soviet Army and Navy Main Political Directorate) responded, "It will be up to the Afghans whether to have advisers or not. If such a request was made, we will consider this request." His statement was hardly a strong commitment.[29] Even the Afghan Marxist leader Najibullah forecast that the number of advisers would be relatively limited.[30] And according to General Boris Gromov, commander of Soviet forces in Afghanistan, the Kabul government has "guaranteed" the safety of Soviet advisers remaining in Afghanistan after the departure of Soviet troops.[31] His statement may imply that if later Kabul could not guarantee their safety, Moscow might then withdraw them.

These statements do not indicate that Gorbachev is forcing the Soviet military to withdraw from Afghanistan despite opposition from his generals. On the contrary, the Soviet military leadership appears quite willing to be relieved of this mission. The defense minister, General Dimitri Yazov, has even held up the Geneva accords on Afghanistan as a model for resolving other regional conflicts.[32] Whether this indicates that he is willing to risk the possible overthrow of other pro-Soviet Marxist regimes is unclear, but does suggest that the highest military leader does not oppose Gorbachev's desire to curtail Soviet military involvement in the defense of weak Marxist regimes.

The Soviets fulfilled their pledge to withdraw half their troops from Afghanistan by August 15, 1988. In November 1988, however, Moscow announced that it was delaying the withdrawal of its remaining troops because of continued external aid to the mujahideen. The Soviets also hinted that the troop withdrawal might be delayed past the agreed-upon date for completion of the pullout (February 15, 1989) unless external aid to the Afghan rebels ceases.[33] More ominously, the Soviets deployed some 30 MiG-27s to Afghanistan and began using Tu-26 ("Backfire") bombers there for the first time. Moscow has also sent Scud missiles to Kabul that can reach targets in Pakistan from Afghan territory.[34]

Rather than signaling that the Soviets had reneged on their promise to withdraw from Afghanistan, these moves were an attempt to reduce external aid to the mujahideen before the completion of the Soviet pullout. The United States stepped up its military activity in Indochina just before its complete withdrawal. This was done to forestall Communist attacks while the withdrawal was taking place as well as to strengthen the regime the United States was defending. Increased Soviet military activity in Afghanistan before the final withdrawal of Soviet forces on February 15, 1989 was probably due to similar motives. Indeed, it seems doubtful that Gorbachev and the Soviet military leadership would want to continue defending the Marxist regime in Kabul after having acknowledged the difficulty of the task themselves and having raised internal as well as external expectations about the coming to an end of direct Soviet military involvement in Afghanistan. It should be noted, however, that Moscow has continued to provide military assistance to Kabul since the February 1989 pullout.

Dissenting Voices

Some Soviet generals have nevertheless made statements indicating a desire to continue Soviet assistance to "progressive" regimes. In April 1987, Lt. General N. Shapalin wrote:

> The Soviet Union gives disinterested assistance to the liberated countries which have embarked on a path of progressive development in defending their territorial integrity, independence, sovereignty, and in strengthening their defense capability, when [these countries] request assistance.[35]

In a January 1988 broadcast of the television program "I Serve the Soviet Union" (in which Defense Minister Yazov appeared), Col. General D. A. Volkogonov, deputy chief of the Main Political Directorate, said, "Appropriately, the Soviet Armed Forces also exist for the purpose of rendering help to progressive regimes and national liberation movements."[36]

Not surprisingly, some voices in the military call for continued Soviet aid to the national liberation movement; Gorbachev's primary rival in the Politburo, Yegor Ligachev, appears to hold this view. Ligachev indicated his desire to continue aiding revolutionary regimes and groups in the

Third World when he stated in August 1988 that "active participation in the solution of universal human problems in no way means any artificial 'deceleration' of social and national liberation struggle."[37] Gorbachev, however, appears to have weakened Ligachev's position, especially his influence on foreign policy, by moving him in October 1988 from his position in charge of ideology to agriculture in the CPSU Central Committee Secretariat.

What is noteworthy, however, is that even before Gorbachev's authority had been more fully consolidated and Ligachev was able to announce his opposition to Soviet retrenchment from the Third World, the general trend in Soviet military thought was supportive of Gorbachev's military policy toward the developing world. In the unlikely event Ligachev suddenly found himself in power, he could still find generals willing to resume active Soviet military aid to Marxist regimes and revolutionary groups; clearly, some do advocate this policy. But as long as Gorbachev or any other Soviet leader in power regards perestroika and peaceful coexistence as the highest priority for the USSR, the Soviet military leadership is unlikely to advocate the aggressive pursuit of positive military goals in the Third World if this threatens more important domestic and foreign policy goals.

3

Gorbachev and Soviet Support for Revolution

Soviet support for revolution has allowed Moscow simultaneously to pursue positive and negative military objectives in the Third World. As discussed in chapter 1, a successful revolution often brought about the immediate achievement of negative military goals: the revolutionary government usually had no desire to ally with the West against the USSR, especially if it came to power with Soviet help and against Western opposition. In military terms, the West would lose whatever military facilities it may have enjoyed under the previous regime. And the revolutionary regime would be unlikely to grant the West military facilities in the future.

At the same time, support for revolution could (but did not always) advance the USSR's positive military goals, though perhaps not as immediately as its negative ones. Beyond denying military facilities to the West, the revolutionary government could grant them to the USSR. With these bases and with strong alliances to revolutionary states generally, Moscow improved its ability to (1) protect the sea lines of communication between the western and eastern USSR, (2) intervene militarily in defense of its revolutionary allies when attacked by internal or external

30

opponents, and (3) assist revolutionaries in neighboring countries.

Before Gorbachev, the Soviets had considerable success in supporting and allying with Third World revolutionaries. Marxists came to power by revolution in China during the 1940s, in North Vietnam and Cuba during the 1950s, in South Yemen during the 1960s, and in South Vietnam, Cambodia, Laos, Ethiopia, Guinea-Bissau, Mozambique, Angola, Afghanistan, Nicaragua, and Grenada during the 1970s. In addition, the Soviets allied with non-Marxist but revolutionary regimes that came to power in Ghana, Guinea, Egypt, and Iraq during the 1950s, and in Algeria, Mali, Libya, Somalia, North Yemen, and Syria during the 1960s. Finally, although the Iranian revolution of the 1970s was not pro-Soviet, it ousted a pro-U.S. regime on the USSR's southern border.

Not all of these countries have remained Soviet allies. The Marxist regime in China split with Moscow during the 1960s, and U.S. intervention ousted the Marxists from Grenada in 1983. Mozambique seems to have drifted away from a pro-Soviet foreign policy orientation. Through either a change in policy or a change in regime, Ghana, Guinea, Guinea-Bissau, Iraq, Algeria, Mali, and North Yemen became increasingly nonaligned while Egypt and Somalia became actively pro-Western. In addition, not all Marxist or other groups supported by the Soviets or their allies have come to power—for example, the failed attempts at Marxist revolution in Malaysia, Bolivia, Colombia, Venezuela, Oman, North Yemen, and elsewhere. In Zimbabwe, Moscow backed one of the two liberation groups vying for power, but not the one that eventually succeeded—a mistake that proved a serious obstacle to Soviet efforts to establish good relations with the victorious Robert Mugabe for several years.

Despite these setbacks, the Soviets have realized a number of enduring benefits through the revolutionary regimes that have remained in power and pro-Soviet. The United States and the West have lost access to these countries as military allies through which they could harm Soviet interests. Three of these countries (Ethiopia, South Yemen, and Vietnam) lie along the strategic SLOC via the Red Sea, Indian Ocean, and Western Pacific between the eastern and western USSR. Angola lies along the South Atlantic SLOC that leads into the Indian Ocean via the Cape of Good Hope. These and other revolutionary states where the USSR has military access increase the Soviet ability to act against Western interests. Moscow's alliance with Cuba has been especially valuable because Cuba provided most of the troops necessary to install and prop up the Popular Movement for the Liberation of Angola (MPLA) regime in Angola as well as drive Somali forces out of Ethiopia's Ogaden region. And even when national liberation movements have been unable to win state power, Soviet aid to them can still benefit Moscow. Soviet support to the Palestine Liberation Organization (PLO), for example, has helped Moscow bolster its position in the Arab world.

Because it is not the purpose of this study to provide a detailed account of Soviet military assistance to national liberation movements before Gorbachev came to power, just the outline of this history will be reviewed here. Stalin abruptly changed Soviet policy to aid revolutionaries on several occasions — for example, by de-emphasizing revolution during 1935–1939 when he feared the rising power of Nazi Germany. He encouraged revolutionaries, however, while he was allied with Hitler during 1939–1941. After Hitler invaded the USSR in 1941, Stalin abruptly changed course again and allied himself with Britain and then the United States. With the onset of the Cold War, however, he returned to calling for revolution in the Third World. Stalin's decision about whether to emphasize or de-emphasize revolution in the Third World, then, was significantly determined by whether he sought to cooperate with or to weaken the West. This, however, was not always the case. In the mid-1920s, the Soviets sought improved relations with the West, but were also supporting revolution in China.[38]

Stalin also varied his policy about what type of revolutionaries to aid. In China, Stalin at first opposed Trotsky's call to back the Chinese Communist Party (CCP). Instead, he backed the more broadly nationalist Kuo Min Tang (KMT) and ordered the CCP to support it as well. When KMT leader Chiang Kai-shek suddenly attacked and substantially weakened the CCP, Stalin then ordered the Chinese Communists to launch an urban rebellion, which was promptly crushed.[39] Stalin was wary of broad-based nationalist movements after this experience and tended to support more orthodox Marxist-Leninist ones later. But it is not clear that he was anxious to see Marxist-Leninists come to power who were not firmly under his control, as his ambivalent policy toward aiding the Chinese Communists after World War II demonstrated. Stalin was not particularly optimistic about the prospects of extending Soviet influence in the Third World generally, and for the most part he assigned it a minor role in Soviet foreign and military policy.

Khrushchev, by contrast, was far more optimistic about the prospects for newly independent states in Asia and Africa to become allied to the USSR. During his tenure in office, Moscow favored more broadly based nationalist revolutionary movements over the more narrowly Marxist-Leninist ones Stalin backed in the late 1940s. Although Khrushchev viewed the former as having a better chance of coming to power than the latter, he gave these groups only limited aid, preferring instead to support anti-Western leaders that came to power on their own. Even when Khrushchev aided national liberation movements, he often did so through other Third World states such as Egypt. He saw the West's position in the Third World as too strong and the need for peaceful coexistence in the nuclear era as too great to risk confrontation with the United States through large-scale Soviet support to national liberation movements.[40]

In the early years of the Brezhnev era, Moscow appeared to reduce its commitment to Third World revolutionaries. Several of the radical civilian leaders whom Khrushchev backed were ousted in military coups. In this period, revolutionary prospects in the Third World seemed weak, and U.S. willingness to suppress such activity—in Indochina, for example—seemed great. The situation changed dramatically during the 1970s, when the U.S. withdrawal from Indochina ushered in a period of U.S. unwillingness to undertake protracted counterinsurgency operations. At the same time, there was an upsurge of revolutionary activity—especially of the Marxist variety—in several countries of the Third World. After the defection of Egypt and Somalia from the Soviet orbit to the U.S. one, many Soviet experts concluded that Marxist-Leninist regimes were more likely to remain loyal Soviet allies than radical non-Marxist ones. At a time when their prospects for success had greatly improved, Moscow was eager to support the more reliable Marxist groups.[41]

Conditions in the 1970s seemed particularly favorable to Soviet support for Marxist revolution. These conditions, however, had changed dramatically by the time Gorbachev came to power. Although Marxist revolutionaries had succeeded in gaining power in several countries during the 1970s, this trend did not continue in other countries during the 1980s. Indeed, the USSR and its allies had to undertake costly efforts to keep in power several of the successful revolutionary groups of the 1970s. Moscow's support to revolutionaries did not halt Washington's willingness to continue progress on arms control during the 1970s until the Soviet invasion of Afghanistan. The Brezhnev leadership apparently concluded that Washington needed arms control more than Moscow did and thus in its period of decline following Vietnam could not afford to make too much of an issue of Soviet behavior in the Third World. Gorbachev, by contrast, has shown that he considers the success of U.S.-Soviet arms control essential to his domestic goals. It is not surprising that Gorbachev has reduced Soviet aid to Third World revolutionaries, given the lack of revolutionary opportunities in the 1980s compared with the 1970s as well as Gorbachev's perception of a greater need for cooperative relations with the West compared with Brezhnev's.

Is Gorbachev's de-emphasis on aiding Marxist revolution permanent or temporary? Would he resume Soviet aid to Third World revolutionaries if U.S.-Soviet relations suddenly deteriorated or if the prospects of national liberation movements suddenly increased? It is impossible, of course, to answer these questions definitively. There are indications, however, that Gorbachev has accepted the arguments of several Soviet civilian academics that socialist revolution is not the "wave of the future" in the Third World while the growing strength and power of non-Marxist capitalist states is.[42]

In previous periods when the USSR de-emphasized aid to national liberation movements, Soviet leaders at least continued to proclaim that doing so was their goal. By contrast, Gorbachev has made very little mention of national liberation movements, though he has spoken at length on issues, such as debt, that are a source of contention between primarily non-Marxist, capitalist-oriented Third World states and the West.[43] In his speech on the seventieth anniversary of the October Revolution, Gorbachev seemed to redefine the concept of national liberation:

> It is customary to talk of the decline of the national liberation movement, but what is going on here, obviously, is a substitution of concepts and a non-recognition of the new nature of the situation. If the liberating impulse which operated at the stage of the struggle for political independence is meant, then it is weakening, of course, and that is natural. But the impulse necessary for the new, present stage of the development of the Third World is only just taking shape; and it is necessary to be clearly aware of this and not to fall into pessimism. The factors from which this impulse is formed are varied and heterogenous. Here there is a powerful economic process which sometimes take on paradoxical forms: for example, some countries retain features of underdevelopment and emerge at the level of great powers in world economics and politics. There is also a growth of political energy in the course of formation of nations and consolidation of national

states in the genuine sense, a considerable place among whom is occupied by countries with revolutionary regimes. There are also grapes of wrath on the soil of the glaring polarization of poverty and wealth and the contrast between possibilities and the real situation. The force of originality and independent action is working in an increasingly pronounced and active way in organizations reflecting the processes of the inter-state consolidation of developing countries.[44]

Here Gorbachev identifies the concerns of non-Marxist, capitalist Third World states with national liberation. He seems to applaud the fact that some states have become "great powers in world economics and politics." But this has really only occurred in capitalist-oriented, not socialist-oriented, countries. He does include "revolutionary regimes" among those nations that have experienced "genuine" consolidation of national states, but does not claim they are the only ones to do so. "Polarization of poverty and wealth" could refer to the division between rich and poor within Third World states, but he does not state this specifically. He could also mean the differences between most Third World states, whether capitalist or socialist, and the West. Finally, the positive reference to organizations reflecting "inter-state consolidation of developing countries" refers mainly to non-Marxist states, because they are the primary ones that have formed regional organizations. Gorbachev has redefined national liberation in a broader and distinctly less revolutionary manner than his predecessors.

Gorbachev has also ended or decided against Soviet support for revolution in several key countries where the success of revolution would definitely advance Soviet military policy. This is particularly true in Oman, the Philippines, and Panama where there are important U.S. military facilities.

During the early 1970s, Moscow gave military assistance via South Yemen to the Marxist Popular Front for the Liberation of Oman (PFLO). Even after this group was defeated in 1975, the Soviets continued to express support for it and to heap invective on the pro-Western Sultan of Oman well into the 1980s. Under Gorbachev, however, the Soviets have not only abandoned any mention of the PFLO, but in September 1985 established diplomatic relations with the sultan's government for the first time.[45] Gorbachev has apparently decided that because revolution is unlikely in Oman, it is foolish to continue giving propaganda support to it. Under these circumstances, the Soviet Union may have a much better chance of reducing U.S. military access to Oman (a negative military goal) by convincing the sultan that Moscow is not a threat to him than by attempting to overthrow him.

In the Philippines, Gorbachev has apparently given no military assistance to the Marxist New People's Army (NPA) despite the increase in this group's strength during the mid-1980s. Although the NPA is not pro-Soviet, its victory would almost certainly lead to the ousting of the United States from the Clark and Subic Bay bases.[46] Instead, the Soviets under Gorbachev expressed their support for Ferdinand Marcos until the time he was ousted with U.S. help.[47] The Soviets may have calculated that Marcos was strong enough to resist pressure to resign from Washington as well as from his internal opponents. Had he done so, U.S.-Philippine relations may have continued to deteriorate, and Marcos may have acted to reduce U.S. military access to the two bases. Soviet relations with Corazon Aquino were strained at first, but during 1987–1988 Moscow attempted to improve relations with her. The Soviets have apparently concluded that their negative military goals are not likely to be achieved by supporting a non-Marxist government's Marxist guerrilla opponents even when they are relatively strong. Soviet aid to the rebels, even if only verbal, might make the Aquino government fearful of the USSR and thus more willing to allow the United States to retain its bases.

Similarly, the Soviets have expressed their support for General Manuel Noriega throughout the period since Washington has attempted to oust him in favor of a democratic government.[48] Here again, Moscow may have calculated that Noriega was strong enough to survive U.S. and internal pressure to resign. If he survives (an increasingly likely prospect), Noriega might attempt to reduce U.S. access to the Panama Canal—a development that would be very much in Soviet interests. It should be noted that even before Gorbachev, the Soviets have had good relations with the "leftist" Panamanian military leaders Omar Torrijos and Noriega. These leaders, however, have not been Marxist and the unpopularity of Noriega certainly provides an opportunity to weaken him. Gorbachev, however, apparently thinks Soviet interests are better served by supporting the existing regime in Panama than by seeking its overthrow.

Elsewhere in Central America, Gorbachev's de-emphasis on revolution is even more dramatic than in Panama. During the early 1980s, Moscow encouraged and may have sanctioned military assistance via Cuba and Nicaragua to Marxist guerrillas in Guatemala and Honduras. Since Gorbachev came to power, however, Moscow has downplayed the role of the rebels and has even tried to improve relations with the governments of these two nations.[49] Gorbachev apparently hopes to weaken the two governments' ties with Washington and thus does not want to give them any incentive to fear the Soviet Union. It would be particularly useful to the Soviets if the Honduran government refused to allow Washington to support the Nicaraguan contras from Honduran territory.

With regard to South Africa, several Soviet academicians have expressed the view since Gorbachev came to power that a violent revolution is not necessary to end apartheid. Instead, they have argued that a peaceful solution is possible that protects the interests of all parties, including the whites.[50]

All these cases show that Gorbachev has certainly de-emphasized military aid to national liberation movements as a prominent feature of Soviet military policy. Nevertheless, he has not ended aid to national liberation movements altogether. The Soviets still give some military support—

and much propaganda support – to the PLO, the African National Congress (ANC), the South African Communist Party (SACP), and the South West Africa People's Organization (SWAPO).[51] Of course, the military assistance Moscow provides these groups has not been enough to give them a serious chance of coming to power. Such aid, however, does help them remain active and avoid defeat by their opponents. Furthermore, the Soviets can contrast their military aid to the PLO, however limited, with large-scale U.S. military assistance to Israel in order to help boost their image with the Arab states. Similarly, the Soviets can contrast their aid to the ANC and SWAPO with the lack of U.S. support for these groups (as well as friendly U.S. relations with Pretoria generally) to project a favorable image of Moscow to black African governments and to blacks in South Africa and Namibia.

Numerous Soviet statements made since Gorbachev has come to power indicate that Moscow hopes to see revolutionary situations develop in certain countries. In Chile, for example, the Soviets urged the non-Communist opposition parties to join in a united front with the Marxist Manuel Rodriguez Patriotic Front in a revolutionary struggle against General Augusto Pinochet. They strove to discredit U.S. efforts to encourage democratization and warned that true democracy was not possible without the participation of the Marxists.[52] If a revolutionary government came to power in Chile and an anti-U.S. government were in power in Panama, there could be important military consequences. The United States would need to devote increased resources to maintaining the SLOCs between its eastern and western coasts – a problem Washington has not had to worry about seriously before. Nevertheless, this prospect appears to be extremely unlikely.

Moscow has also warned that Washington intended to replace General Alfredo Stroessner with the facade of a "bourgeois democracy" in Paraguay. The Soviets insisted that only a revolutionary struggle involving the Communist Party can bring true democracy to Paraguay.[53] In addition, Soviet commentary refuses to acknowledge that free elections or democratic institutions exist in El Salvador. Moscow constantly characterizes the government of José Napoleón Duarte as a military dictatorship and insists that the only acceptable settlement to the conflict involves power sharing with the Marxist guerrillas. Moscow claims that the Duarte government's call for the Marxists to participate in free elections is a sham.[54] Yet even if there were revolution in El Salvador, the Soviets might not gain any significant additional military benefit besides those they already enjoy in Nicaragua. A Marxist regime in Paraguay might provide the USSR with no military advantages whatsoever but only induce heightened fear of Moscow as well as cooperation with Washington in the more important neighboring countries.

Although some Soviet scholars have stated that a peaceful transition to black majority rule in South Africa is possible, under Gorbachev numerous Soviet radio broadcasts have warned black South Africans that such a transition can come about only through revolution. Moscow has claimed that Western calls for a peaceful transition to black majority rule are duplicitous. The United States and others are said to offer these proposals solely as a means of dividing the black opposition and perpetuating white minority rule.[55] Given that South Africa is the most important country in Black Africa, a Marxist revolution there could certainly provide important military advantages to the USSR even if neighboring black states became frightened of Moscow. The Soviets might be in a stronger position to deny Western access to the many strategic minerals that are located exclusively or predominantly in South Africa.

Nevertheless, although Gorbachev may be encouraging revolutionary situations to develop in Chile, Paraguay, El Salvador, and South Africa, he is not committing many Soviet resources toward that end. Instead he seems to be ensuring that revolutionary options are not foreclosed by democratic or peaceful solutions to the causes of conflict in these countries. In addition, Gorbachev seems careful to give verbal support for revolution in those countries where the government is particularly unpopular regionally or internationally. In other words, Moscow is calling for the overthrow of governments primarily when doing so enhances Moscow's standing with neighboring countries. The Soviets aim not only to avoid threatening these states and pushing them to seek U.S. protection, but also to identify the United States with the unpopular regime as well as with threats to their security. By providing these revolutionaries only a small amount of actual military assistance but generous verbal support, Gorbachev may seek to allay the fears of non-Marxist states as well as to avoid complicating U.S.-Soviet relations.

It is impossible to say whether Gorbachev might increase Soviet assistance to Third World revolutionaries if conditions again favor revolution as they did in the 1970s. Gorbachev's actions and statements indicate, however, that he does not expect conditions to become favorable for revolution again in the foreseeable future. Except in certain special situations, then, even rhetorical Soviet support for revolution is counterproductive because it is unlikely to succeed and because it can harm other goals, such as perestroika and détente, that Gorbachev values highly. Furthermore, supporting Marxist revolution can be extremely costly to the USSR if the Marxists come to power but need substantial external assistance to remain there, as has been the case in Afghanistan, Cambodia, Ethiopia, Angola, Mozambique, and Nicaragua. Finally, strong support for revolution could be counterproductive to Gorbachev's efforts to improve relations with the most important non-Marxist Third World states. And, as will be discussed in Chapter 5, improving Soviet relations with non-Marxist states may be a far more effective means of pursuing negative Soviet military goals than supporting Marxist revolution.

4

Defending Marxist
Third World Regimes

What does the Soviet withdrawal from Afghanistan mean for Soviet policy toward other Third World Marxist regimes fighting externally backed insurgents? Gorbachev and many other high-level Soviet officials have declared that the Geneva accords on Afghanistan could serve as a model for resolving other regional conflicts. Does this mean that Gorbachev is prepared to withdraw Soviet support for other Third World Marxist regimes? This course would be quite different from de-emphasizing revolution. By not supporting Marxist revolutionaries, Gorbachev would sacrifice only the potential positive and negative military goals the USSR may have achieved had they been successful. But by withdrawing support from existing Marxist Third World regimes, Gorbachev would risk losing whatever actual positive and negative military goals the USSR has already gained.

Different Third World Marxist states, of course, do not all serve the same Soviet military objectives (nor necessarily any military objectives). To the extent that they do serve similar goals, each may do so to a greater or lesser degree than the others. Also, Gorbachev may not value as highly as his predecessors the military objectives that some Third World Marxist states served. Chapter 3 concluded that

Gorbachev does not consider Marxist revolution the "wave of the future" in the Third World. If this is indeed the case, Gorbachev does not need Marxist Third World regimes to serve as bases from which the USSR can support revolution in neighboring countries. And because Gorbachev has placed greater emphasis on improving relations with non-Marxist states, Soviet use of existing Marxist states to spread revolution in the Third World would hinder this goal.

Afghanistan is another example. Brezhnev's motives for intervening there are still not entirely clear. Some have argued, especially around the time of the 1979 intervention, that the Soviets valued Afghanistan as a base to facilitate the achievement of more ambitious military goals – for example, obtaining a warm-water port on the Indian Ocean or controlling the oil-rich Persian Gulf region upon which the West so heavily depends.[56] Others, such as Francis Fukuyama, have argued that the Soviets intervened in Afghanistan primarily for political reasons: they did not want a Marxist regime on their own border to be overthrown.[57] But whether the primary reason for intervening and later remaining in Afghanistan was military or political, Gorbachev has clearly decided that this goal was not worth the many costs of continued pursuit, given the low probability of easily subduing the Afghan mujahideen.

Nevertheless, there are other Soviet military objectives served by various Third World Marxist regimes that Gorbachev may value pursuing. Three such states – Vietnam, South Yemen, and Ethiopia – lie along the strategic SLOC running through the Indian Ocean between the eastern and western USSR. Without military facilities in these or other countries along this route, maintaining significant amounts of force at the eastern and western ends of the Indian Ocean would be more problematic. These facilities also contribute to the peacetime maintenance of Soviet ASW, reconnaissance, SLOC protection, and other missions. Although the Soviets might have great difficulty in protecting this SLOC in the event of a general war with the United States, they could protect it with their present Indian Ocean military facilities in the event of a war with China. Because China could disrupt the USSR's few land lines of communication to Siberia relatively easily, protecting this SLOC during a conflict with China could be vital to Soviet interests.

Preserving a pro-Soviet Marxist regime in Angola may also serve Moscow's larger military objectives. Although arguably less important than their facilities in Vietnam, Ethiopia, and South Yemen, the Soviets continue to use naval and air facilities in Angola.[58] Despite Cuban agreement to withdraw its troops, Angola could serve as a base to protect an alternate SLOC around the west coast of Africa if Soviet access to the Red Sea via the Suez Canal were cut off or limited by Egypt. In addition, although the Soviets under Gorbachev appear to have little expectation of further revolution occurring in the Third World generally, they continue to regard Namibia and South Africa as exceptions with some revolutionary potential. An ongoing alliance with Angola could allow the USSR and its allies to help pro-Soviet Marxist elements if revolution does develop.

It may be that the continuation of Marxist regimes in Cuba and Nicaragua is primarily of political benefit to the Soviets. Nevertheless, Cuba does provide facilities for Soviet warships in the Caribbean and a reconnaissance post for monitoring U.S. military movements. According to the 1988 edition of the U.S. Department of Defense's *Soviet Military Power*,

> use of Cuban and Nicaraguan facilities by forward-deployed Soviet forces to threaten U.S. sea lines of communication in the Gulf of Mexico, Caribbean Sea, and Panama Canal would complicate U.S. defense planning for contingencies or conflicts in Europe and the Persian Gulf, and force the United States to divert resources from other areas.[59]

Although Cuba and Nicaragua have some military value to the USSR, Soviet military capability would not seriously suffer if Moscow lost these two allies.

Vietnam and Cuba have had a special relationship with the Soviets for many years. And they are not facing armed internal opposition as some of the newer Third World Marxist regimes have. The Soviets, then, do not face the choice of supporting continued counterinsurgency operations or risking the downfall of these two governments. But to a greater or lesser degree, Gorbachev has faced this choice in all the other Third World Marxist regimes. What policy will Gorbachev pursue toward these other Marxist regimes that, like Afghanistan, have required significant external support to remain in power? Does the withdrawal from Afghanistan indicate that Gorbachev would be willing to withdraw Soviet support for other beleaguered Marxist Third World regimes? To answer these questions, it is necessary to examine Soviet statements regarding each case individually.

Cambodia

Gorbachev has continued to provide very high levels of military support to Vietnam; Moscow gave Hanoi more than a billion dollars worth of weapons in 1985, 1986, and 1987. The Vietnamese undoubtedly used much of this aid to support their counterinsurgency efforts in Cambodia. Gorbachev has also provided significant military support to Phnom Penh.[60] Nevertheless, there have been signs recently that Gorbachev seeks to cut the costs of this operation by encouraging the Vietnamese to withdraw from Cambodia.

The Soviets have called for a peaceful resolution of conflicts in Southeast Asia for many years. The type of settlement Moscow envisioned when Gorbachev first came to power, however, was a nonaggression pact between Indochina and ASEAN. The war in Kampuchea would then end because ASEAN and other outside parties would cease aiding the Cambodian opposition groups. Vietnamese forces would withdraw from Cambodia, but the Heng Samrin government was to remain in power.[61] Moscow would not even consider the possibility of its sharing power, as was shown by *Pravda*'s hostile reaction to the 1986 proposal by the three Cambodian opposition groups for a quadripartite coalition government:

> It is perfectly clear that the Cambodian problem has already been resolved by the Khmer people themselves. It has been resolved definitively and irreversibly. To ignore that objective fact, to fail to see the existence of the sovereign state of the PRK, and to deny that it is the sole legitimate representative of the Cambodian people is like trying to measure the sky with a bamboo pole, as they say in Asia. But no one has managed to do that yet.[62]

But even in 1985 – and with increasing frequency later – Moscow called for talks between the People's Republic of Kampuchea (PRK) and the two non-Communist opposition groups. The "Pol Potists," however, were to be excluded from any discussions as well as from any share of power.[63] Soviet statements also gave much publicity to Hanoi's declaration that it would withdraw all Vietnamese troops from Cambodia by 1990. Especially since 1987, Soviet statements have emphasized the need for national reconciliation in Cambodia.[64] In May 1987, Gorbachev stated at a dinner for Vietnamese party leader Nguyen Van Linh that the Cambodian problem "can only be solved proceeding from the highest interests of the Cambodian people and their legitimate right to shape their destiny themselves, on the basis of the unification of all their national patriotic forces."[65]

In 1988, Soviet statements placed even greater emphasis on the possibility of a negotiated settlement in Cambodia that would involve some form of power sharing by the Heng Samrin government as well as the withdrawal of Vietnamese troops. The increasing Soviet support for such action appears to accompany greater willingness on the part of Hanoi to extract itself from the conflict, as indicated in its announcement that 50,000 Vietnamese troops and the Vietnamese military headquarters would be withdrawn from Phnom Penh by the end of 1988.[66]

As A. M. Dryukov (the Soviet ambassador to Singapore) noted, the USSR cannot compel Vietnam to settle the Cambodian issue.[67] But Moscow's increasing encouragement of a peaceful settlement and praise for Vietnam's withdrawal plans demonstrate that Gorbachev does not oppose these moves—indeed he actively supports them. Nor did the Soviet military object to reducing the Soviet-Vietnamese commitment in Cambodia; as one *Krasnaya Zvezda* article noted, "There can be no military solution."[68]

Soviet statements, however, indicate that there is disagreement within the Soviet leadership about the participation of the Khmer Rouge in any future Cambodian government. Most Soviet statements have condemned the "Pol Potists" and have explicitly stated that the Khmer Rouge, or at least Pol Pot and his closest associates, must be excluded from any peace settlement.[69] But one Soviet commentary cited PRK Prime Minister Hun Sen as saying, "A complete solution is possible only when the Pol Pot group agrees to take part in the political process of building peace. If it refuses, the problem can only be partly solved."[70] Other Soviet statements seem to leave open the possibility that the Khmer Rouge can take part in the settlement.[71]

The evolution of Soviet statements on Cambodia since 1985 indicate that the Gorbachev leadership has become increasingly less committed to defending a pro-Soviet, pro-Vietnamese regime in Cambodia. As in Afghanistan, the cost of propping up the regime no longer appears worth the effort in Soviet eyes. The Soviets do not wish to see a government hostile to Vietnam come to power in Cambodia, but they seem to have become more willing to take such a risk to end Moscow's and Hanoi's expensive involvement in the conflict.

Angola

Under Gorbachev, the Soviets have apparently increased their military aid to the MPLA regime in Angola. Moscow gave Luanda military assistance valued at $775 million in

1985, $1,200 million in 1986 and $1,500 million in 1987.[72] In addition, Soviet military advisers have reportedly taken a greater role in combat operations since Gorbachev came to power than they ever did before.[73] In 1988, Cuban troops in Angola numbered 35,000–50,000 – a level even higher than the initial Cuban intervention to save the MPLA and defeat its opponents in 1975–1976. With Soviet and Cuban help, the MPLA expanded its area of operations nearly to the Namibian border.[74]

The Soviets have also called for a peaceful resolution to the conflict in Angola. Indeed, Cuba, Angola, South Africa, and the United States (with Moscow's blessing) signed peace accords for Angola and Namibia in December 1988. The accords call for Namibian independence, South African withdrawal from Angola and Namibia, and Cuban withdrawal from Angola. But this Cuban withdrawal will only occur 15 months after the withdrawal of South African forces from Namibia. The South African withdrawal is to be completed by April 1990 while the Cubans have until July 1991 to quit Angola.[75] Moscow, Havana, and Luanda refused, however, to negotiate with the National Union for the Total Independence of Angola (UNITA) or to allow UNITA any role in the Angolan peace talks.[76] Nor is there any question of the MPLA's entering talks on national reconciliation with UNITA. At most, Luanda is willing to offer amnesty to surrendering UNITA soldiers.[77]

It is unclear how committed Gorbachev would be to defending Marxism in Angola if the MPLA were as weak as the Marxist regimes in Afghanistan or Cambodia. But this is not the case. Soviet statements about Angola indicate that Moscow does not see the MPLA as being seriously threatened by UNITA or regard the effort to defend the MPLA as particularly burdensome. Unlike the Marxist regimes in Kabul and Phnom Penh, it appears that the Gorbachev leadership expects the MPLA to remain in power in Luanda and perhaps even to defeat UNITA as a result of the peace settlement for this country.

Ethiopia

The Soviets under Gorbachev have continued giving substantial military and economic assistance to Ethiopia. They have also continued to make use of naval facilities in the Dahlak Islands. Although Gorbachev has not given as much military aid to Addis Ababa as the Soviet leaders did in 1983 and 1984 ($975 million and $1,200 million respectively), he did provide $800 million in 1985. In 1986, the Soviets gave only $310 million, but provided substantially more in 1987.[78]

From 1985 through 1987, the Soviet media said almost nothing about the regional insurgencies confronting the Marxist regime in Ethiopia. In 1988, however, Soviet coverage of Ethiopia increased. Moscow praised the Somali-Ethiopian peace agreement in which each side agreed to cease subversive activity against the other; it was seen as a fine example of the peaceful resolution of conflicts.[79] There was also frank acknowledgment not only that the rebels were continuing their operations in Eritrea and Tigre, but that they had recently launched successful offensives against Ethiopian forces. These commentators claimed that Addis Ababa had previously offered to negotiate with the rebels, but the rebels rejected the offer. Far from advocating a peaceful resolution to the conflicts, these articles implied that such a solution was no longer possible.[80] That this was indeed the view of the Gorbachev leadership was implied in a commentary about Karen Brutents's delivering a message from Gorbachev to Ethiopian leader Mengistu Haile Mariam in Asmara (the largest city in Eritrea):

> A common conviction was expressed that the way to the elimination of tension in the area in the Horn of Africa lies through solution to the existing problems by political means on the basis of the principles of *territorial integrity of states*, non-interference in their internal affairs on the part of external forces, and the development of good neighborly relations.[81]

Referring to territorial integrity of states implied that Moscow supported Mengistu's efforts to prevent Eritrean and Tigrean guerrillas from disrupting it. Soviet statements do not indicate that Moscow considers that the principle of national reconciliation applies to the secessionist conflicts within this country. Instead, they suggest that Gorbachev is committed not only to preserving the pro-Soviet regime in Addis Ababa, but also to assisting it to regain control of territory that has been overrun by secessionist guerrillas.

Nicaragua

Gorbachev has continued to give substantial military assistance to Managua. In 1986, Moscow gave it an unprecedented $575 million worth of arms.[82] Under Gorbachev, Soviet commentary on Nicaragua has for the most part echoed the views of the Sandinista leadership. There has been some acknowledgment of internal causes of instability, but the primary cause is "external counterrevolution, organized, supported, and egged on by the United States and backed by Central America's reactionary circles."[83]

Moscow, however, has not opposed peace efforts in Central America. Under Gorbachev, the Soviets aligned themselves with the Contadora process and later with the Arias plan (which the Central American states agreed to in Guatemala in August 1987). The particular feature of the Guatemala accords that Moscow approved was that of ending external assistance to opposition groups in Nicaragua. But Moscow initially supported Managua's reluctance to enter talks with the internal opposition as called for by the accords.[84]

At a February 1988 meeting between Soviet Foreign Minister Eduard Shevardnadze and Nicaraguan Foreign Minister Miguel D'Escoto, however, it appeared that Moscow was encouraging Managua to enter talks with the contras—which they did a few weeks later.[85] But while Moscow praised Managua for pursuing "national reconciliation" efforts, Soviet statements clearly indicated that the Kremlin did not expect the Sandinistas to share power with the contras. As in Angola, the primary concession to the opposition was to be amnesty. If the contras did not accept peace on Managua's terms, however, the Soviets approvingly quoted Nicaraguan President Daniel Ortega to the effect that "the Somozist hirelings would be wiped out."[86] Gorbachev himself also indicated that the USSR would stop arms shipments to Nicaragua only if the United States agreed to halt them to other Central American states.[87]

It is highly unlikely that Brezhnev, much less Gorbachev, would have sanctioned Soviet or Cuban military intervention to protect the Sandinistas. Soviet statements about Nicaragua since 1985, however, suggest that the Gorbachev leadership does not regard the contras as a serious threat to the Sandinistas, especially at present. They also reveal that Gorbachev is likely to continue the present level of Soviet military support to Nicaragua if necessary, and that he regards the threat posed by the contras as significantly diminishing.

Mozambique

Gorbachev has sharply reduced the level of Soviet arms transfers to Mozambique. Although Moscow gave Maputo military assistance valued at $400 million in 1983 and $360 million in 1984, Gorbachev reduced it to $270 million in 1985 and $170 million in 1986.[88] This amount is far less than what he has provided to Angola and even to Nicaragua.

Since Gorbachev came to power, there has been relatively little Soviet discussion of the South African-backed insurgency of the Mozambique National Resistance (RENAMO) against Mozambique's Marxist government (Mozambique Liberation Front or FRELIMO). This may be partly because Soviet-Mozambican relations are complicated: although Maputo has good relations with Moscow, it also has good relations with the West generally. What little Soviet commentary there has been indicates that the Gorbachev leadership supports FRELIMO's position of not negotiating with RENAMO at all but only offering amnesty to rebels who surrender.[89] One Radio Moscow broadcast in Portuguese stated that there was no similarity between the situations in Afghanistan and Mozambique: "The situation in Mozambique is different. There is no liberation movement. There is no organized movement. There is simply a war promoted by South Africa."[90]

The Gorbachev leadership may be advocating that Mozambique not negotiate with the rebels because Moscow does not consider RENAMO a serious threat to FRELIMO. But Moscow may have also adopted this hardline position to retain what influence it has in Maputo. Although Mozambique has improved its ties with the West, it has continued to seek Soviet military assistance so long as the war continues. If the May 1988 South African–Mozambican revival of the 1984 Nkmomati accords really leads to a cessation in South African aid to RENAMO, Mozambique will offer even less opportunity for the USSR to gain influence.[91] FRELIMO might then have no reason to depend on the USSR for anything and thus might move even closer to the West. The Kremlin might believe that prolonging the war would prevent such a situation. In any event, Soviet statements about Mozambique do not suggest that Gorbachev wishes to end all Soviet military support for Mozambique.

South Yemen

Gorbachev has demonstrated his desire to defend Soviet access to South Yemen not only by continuing arms transfers to that country, but by militarily intervening in the short civil war between rival pro-Soviet Marxist factions that erupted in January 1986. According to the U.S. Department of Defense, Soviet pilots flew combat missions for the hard-line faction that prevailed. In addition, the Soviets airlifted a battalion of Cuban troops to South Yemen, which led the final attack that drove the previous leader, 'Ali Nasir Muhammad, and his supporters over the border into North Yemen. Soviet naval units also intervened on the side of 'Ali Nasir's opponents.[92]

The Soviets provided South Yemen with $390 million worth of arms in 1985 and $280 million in 1986.[93] This amount is relatively modest compared with Soviet aid to Angola or Nicaragua, but the Marxists in South Yemen have not had to fight a protracted anti-Soviet insurgency as have other Marxist Third World regimes. Indeed, one of the reasons that the Soviets may have intervened in the South Yemeni civil war was to prevent non-Marxist forces from taking advantage of the intraparty fighting to overthrow Marxist rule altogether. Since the fighting stopped, the Soviets have reportedly shipped large quantities of weapons to South Yemen, and military contacts between Moscow and Aden have intensified.[94]

Since the 1986 civil war, Soviet writing about South Yemen appears to be a throwback to the Brezhnev era. The ousted leader, 'Ali Nasir Muhammad, has been criticized for retreating from strict socialism—something that Gorbachev himself is trying to do. The Soviets instead applauded the new leftist leadership's "determination to deepen the revolutionary process of socialist orientation . . . fighting all manifestations of rightist inclinations not only in the sphere of ideology, but in economic policy as well."[95] The Gorbachev leadership not only seems determined to retain South Yemen as an ally, but also appears to think that this is best achieved through supporting the unreformed, ideologically orthodox wing of the Yemeni Socialist Party.

Conclusion

Despite the Soviet withdrawal from Afghanistan, Moscow's actions and statements from 1985 to the present indicate

that Gorbachev does value the preservation of some Marxist Third World regimes. A large part of Gorbachev's motive
may be political: the Soviet Union could increasingly be
perceived as a weakening power if several Marxist regimes
were allowed to be overthrown.

Yet several of the Marxist regimes that Gorbachev has
acted to protect do serve Soviet military objectives, especially those Marxist regimes that lie along Moscow's strategic SLOC through the Indian Ocean. Despite the declining
Soviet naval presence since 1985 in the Indian Ocean and
waters distant from the USSR generally, there is evidence
that the Gorbachev leadership is seriously planning for the
contingency of conflict with China for which protecting the
Indian Ocean SLOC would be vital. Under Gorbachev, the
Soviets have upgraded their naval and air facilities at Cam
Ranh Bay — an important base from which the Soviets could
escort freighters to Vladivostok, attack targets in southern
China by air, and provide offensive or defensive military
support to Vietnam. And Gorbachev has apparently not
slowed the Soviet Union's expensive naval ship-building
plans. Despite the decreased Soviet naval presence in distant waters at present, Gorbachev is apparently retaining
the option to increase it in the future.[96]

Although an obvious point, it should be noted that the
Soviet withdrawal from Afghanistan does not diminish Soviet ability to protect its Indian Ocean SLOC. Because
Marxist rule in Vietnam is secure (there is no significant
armed opposition movement fighting to overthrow the Hanoi regime) and because Soviet access to military facilities
in Vietnam is also secure, the Soviets do not need Cambodia
for their larger SLOC protection goals in the eastern Indi-
an/western Pacific oceans. Because Cambodia, like Afghanistan, has proven difficult and costly to subdue, Gorbachev
is willing to see the Vietnamese cut their losses and withdraw from there as long as the Soviets keep their bases in
Vietnam. And because the security threat that Vietnam
faces from China is not likely to decrease (it would increase
if the Khmer Rouge return to power in Cambodia), Hanoi is
unlikely to expel Moscow's military presence.

At the western end of the Indian Ocean, the situation is different. The military facilities Moscow has in Ethiopia and South Yemen are relatively near each other and thus might seem redundant. But as shown by the ongoing fighting in Eritrea and the 1986 civil war in South Yemen, Marxist rule in these countries and Soviet access to their military facilities is not as secure as in Vietnam. The Gorbachev leadership might consider it prudent to maintain a presence in both countries because neither is completely stable. Also, the USSR and its allies incur much lower costs in preserving pro-Soviet Marxist regimes in these two countries than in Afghanistan or Cambodia. It is not surprising, therefore, that Gorbachev seems intent upon maintaining the Soviet presence in Ethiopia and South Yemen.

Angola does not appear to have the same military importance to Moscow as do Ethiopia, South Yemen, and certainly Vietnam. Apparently, the Soviets and the Cubans would like to reduce the costs of preserving the MPLA regime, as Havana's agreement to withdraw Cuban troops from Angola indicates. But by insisting that South African troops withdraw from Namibia first, Moscow and Havana show that they wish to reduce the risk of the MPLA's being overthrown after the Cuban withdrawal. If the South Africans withdraw from Namibia, they will not be able to support UNITA nearly as effectively as they do now. Moscow and Havana may calculate that a South African withdrawal from Namibia would lead to the defeat of UNITA. Beyond this, the USSR and its allies would be in a much better position to assist the coming to power of SWAPO in Namibia and perhaps increased activity by the ANC and the SACP in South Africa itself.

Cuba contributed to positive Soviet military objectives in the 1970s through its willingness to send large numbers of troops to support Marxist revolutionaries in Angola and Ethiopia. Because Gorbachev has de-emphasized revolution, Cuban support now is not only less useful but less desirable. Cuban leader Fidel Castro himself scaled back Cuba's contribution to helping Ethiopia suppress its regional insurgencies before Gorbachev.[97] If Castro withdraws Cuban forces from Angola, the Cuban contribution to the achievement of Soviet military goals will be even further reduced.

How much does Gorbachev value the contribution of Third World Marxist regimes other than Afghanistan and Cambodia to Soviet military objectives? The answer will not be clear until the threat to other Marxist regimes escalates dramatically. It seems inconceivable in the foreseeable future that significant internal opposition will arise in Cuba or Vietnam: Gorbachev is unlikely to be faced with fighting an unwinnable war to defend Marxist regimes in either Hanoi or Havana. In addition, the effort necessary to defend Marxist regimes in South Yemen, Ethiopia, and Angola — all of which contribute to the achievement of positive Soviet military goals — is much less than the effort to defend them in Afghanistan or Cambodia. And although neither Nicaragua nor Mozambique has much, if any, military importance to the USSR, their Marxist regimes do not face as serious an internal threat as others do. It is relatively inexpensive to keep them in power. The continuation of Sandinista rule despite U.S. opposition is of great propaganda value to Moscow, especially in Latin America. Nevertheless, if the internal opposition in Nicaragua and Mozambique did manage to overthrow the Marxist regimes there, Soviet military capabilities would not be affected significantly.

If, however, opposition forces grew stronger in South Yemen or Ethiopia and if Gorbachev were not willing to make sufficient efforts to defend the Marxist regimes there, it would mean that Gorbachev was not strongly committed to defending the important SLOC between the eastern and western USSR. This would be a highly significant change in Soviet military policy. Similarly, if the USSR and its allies were unwilling to defend the MPLA against a more powerful UNITA, it would indicate that Moscow did not value military facilities in Angola or expect pro-Soviet revolution in southern Africa.

It may be that Gorbachev would be unwilling to support a massive counterinsurgency effort elsewhere in the

Third World if he concluded that such an effort would damage his more important domestic and foreign policy goals. But what is evident from Soviet actions and statements since 1985 is that Gorbachev is working to create conditions under which the USSR will not have to choose between supporting a massive counterinsurgency effort or accepting the overthrow of a Marxist regime in countries other than Afghanistan and Cambodia. To the extent that the USSR is successful in promoting regional peace settlements and "national reconciliation," Gorbachev seeks to limit and eventually eliminate the domestic appeal of the opposition forces fighting against Marxist regimes as well as the external assistance they receive. If he achieves this goal, Gorbachev could retain Marxist Third World regimes as allies while reducing military support to them. The Soviet withdrawal from Afghanistan, then, does not mean that Gorbachev is willing to abandon all other Marxist Third World regimes or relinquish the positive Soviet military objectives they serve.

5

Non-Marxist Third World States and Soviet Military Goals

Gorbachev's predecessors have sought to achieve both positive and negative military goals in non-Marxist Third World states, as they have in Marxist Third World regimes. Not only have the Soviets worked to eliminate Western use of military facilities in non-Marxist Third World countries, but they have also attempted to gain military facilities in them for Soviet use. Traditionally, the maximum Soviet goal in non-Marxist Third World states has been to transform them into exclusive allies of the Soviet Union, ending or preventing any Western military relationship with them. A less ambitious goal has been to neutralize non-Marxist states so that they do not act as allies of the West even if they do not become Soviet allies. The minimum Soviet goal has been to deprive the West of exclusive military relationships with non-Marxist states that are pro-Western. And, of course, to the extent that the Soviets could achieve one of the lesser goals, they have hoped to be in a better position to achieve their more ambitious ones.

It is not the purpose of this chapter to recount the history of Soviet successes and failures in pursuing their positive and negative military goals in non-Marxist Third World states. Moscow certainly experienced both success and failure before Gorbachev came to power. In several instances, Moscow obtained its maximum goal of transforming non-Marxist states into exclusive allies granting base rights to the USSR – at least for a time. Moscow, for example, obtained a greater or lesser degree of military access to bases in Egypt, Syria, Algeria, Iraq, Somalia, Guinea, and other countries. These facilities helped the Soviets in achieving important positive military goals. The facilities in Egypt and later Syria were instrumental in helping the Soviets maintain a naval presence in the Mediterranean. In addition, Soviet bases in Egypt and Somalia were links along vital points of the strategic SLOC running between the eastern and western USSR via the Red Sea and Indian Ocean. Finally, military access to non-Marxist states has aided Soviet military intervention elsewhere in the Third World. The Soviets used facilities in Egypt, for example, to assist the North Yemeni republicans (1962–1968). They also used facilities in Algeria, Guinea, and the Congo to aid the MPLA in Angola (1975–1976) and facilities in South Yemen to help Ethiopia during the Ogaden war (1977–1978).

The Soviets have transferred arms to several non-Marxist states to achieve military as well as political and economic goals. In return for large quantities of arms, for example, they have received access to military facilities in some non-Marxist states. Soviet arms transfers to moderate non-Marxist states generally, including many important such states in the Middle East, have been aimed at preventing the United States and the West from enjoying exclusive military relations with them.

Perhaps the most important factor that has helped the Soviets achieve their positive and negative military goals in these countries is the support these countries have often sought in their disputes or rivalry with Western nations or with other non-Marxist states strongly supported by the United States and the West. Egypt and Syria, for example, granted military facilities to the USSR in return for Soviet military assistance in their conflicts with U.S.-backed Israel. Similarly, the Soviets gained military facilities in Somalia in exchange for building up that country's military strength vis-à-vis U.S.-backed Ethiopia. And Moscow gained access to the Iraqi port of Basra in exchange for building up Iraq's military might vis-à-vis the U.S.-backed Shah of Iran and the conservative Arab states. U.S. military aid to Pakistan was an important reason why India signed a treaty of friendship and cooperation with the USSR in 1971. Increased confrontation between Libya on the one hand and the United States and its allies on the other led to increased Libyan reliance on Soviet military assistance.

Nevertheless, Gorbachev's predecessors experienced several setbacks in attempting to pursue their military objectives in non-Marxist Third World states. These setbacks resulted from seven recurrent problems:

1. Non-Marxist states in Latin America, Africa, the Arabian Peninsula, Southeast Asia, and elsewhere have feared the Soviet Union's efforts to promote revolution against them or neighboring states. Perceiving the USSR as a threat to their survival, they have sought U.S. aid, even when the United States has undertaken actions they disapprove of.

2. Although the USSR has given substantial military assistance to some countries, it has also given military assistance to their regional rivals. This led Somalia to rupture relations with the Soviets. In less extreme cases, non-Marxist Third World governments have found this Soviet practice threatening and have sometimes turned back to the West for arms. At minimum, this practice has made some non-Marxist governments view the USSR as an unreliable ally.

3. Some non-Marxist governments receiving Soviet military aid have been overthrown (for example, in Indonesia, Peru, and several West African states), and the USSR has lost all or most of its influence there.

4. Soviet military assistance is sometimes regarded by non-Marxist Third World governments as insufficient to meet their aims. President Anwar Sadat initially expelled Soviet advisers from Egypt in 1972 because Moscow would

not provide him with the level of arms that he wanted while making extensive use of Egyptian military facilities for Soviet purposes.

5. Some non-Marxist governments that had turned to the USSR for military support because they perceived the West as a threat later improved their ties to the West. Algeria's initial anti-Western sentiments led it to seek Soviet military aid. It still buys Soviet weapons, but its relations with the West have improved. Algeria has been buying Western weapons recently.

6. Several pro-Western Third World states have regarded Soviet regional security proposals as extremely threatening to their security if implemented, often because Soviet proposals favored one side in a conflict – such as the Arab side of the Arab-Israeli conflict. This has led the other side in the conflict, such as Israel, to reject Soviet proposals and to seek U.S. military assistance.

7. Although they have received Soviet military assistance, many states have also sought Western military and economic assistance. Even if they did not fear that the Soviets would work for their overthrow and replacement by a more pro-Soviet regime, they have had no desire to increase Soviet access to their countries and thereby harm their cooperative relations with the West.

Several of these recurrent problems were caused by events over which the Soviets exercised little control, such as coups d'état and outbreaks of conflict. Nevertheless, the manner in which Gorbachev's predecessors – especially Brezhnev – pursued Soviet military objectives in the Third World was often counterproductive. It is easy to understand why a non-Marxist state failed to be persuaded by Soviet arguments that the USSR was its friend and that military relations with the United States were harmful when at the same time Moscow was supporting Marxist revolutionaries, a Marxist regime, or a rival non-Marxist regime in a neighboring country. Similarly, Brezhnev's success in achieving the positive military goal of obtaining military facilities hindered Soviet ability to achieve the negative military goal of reducing U.S. access to military facilities. When Moscow obtained a base in one country, its regional rivals often felt threatened and wanted the United States to retain or even increase its military presence in the region. In short, Soviet efforts to pursue positive and negative military goals simultaneously limited the degree to which Moscow could achieve the latter. And, of course, retaining positive military gains was often problematic: non-Marxist regimes sometimes expelled the Soviets; Marxist regimes were often weak internally and hence costly to maintain in power.

Gorbachev has de-emphasized (though not eliminated) the pursuit of positive goals in Soviet military policy toward the Third World. Gorbachev is no longer trying to acquire new Marxist allies by supporting revolution. And he is trying to reduce the cost of retaining the positive military goals the Soviets have achieved in some Marxist states by promoting regional security agreements. He is even willing to abandon those Marxist allies that are very costly to maintain in power and that contribute only marginally or not at all to Soviet military objectives.

Similarly, Gorbachev has de-emphasized the achievement of positive military goals in non-Marxist states. He has not attempted to transform additional non-Marxist Third World states into exclusive Soviet allies as did Khrushchev and Brezhnev. And although Gorbachev does not want to lose those firm non-Marxist allies that the Soviets already have, he has made clear that he will not support them, as Brezhnev often did, to the extent that they can freely attack their neighbors. Certain Marxist allies have proven costly to the USSR because they were weak internally; considerable effort had to be made to keep them in power. Yet certain radical non-Marxist allies have also proven costly to Moscow because they have used their military assistance from the USSR to attack their neighbors, thus involving the USSR in regional conflicts and complicating Moscow's relations with the West.

Gorbachev has de-emphasized the pursuit of positive

military objectives in the Third World, but he has not de-emphasized the pursuit of negative ones. He has vigorously pursued a policy of attempting to deny U.S. military access to additional bases and to deprive the United States of those bases it already has. Furthermore, Gorbachev has sought to achieve this negative military goal in a more coherent way than his predecessors did by avoiding counterproductive behavior. By de-emphasizing aid to Marxist revolutionaries and even withdrawing aid to some beleaguered Marxist governments, Gorbachev may hope to improve his ability to convince non-Marxist governments that the Soviet Union does not threaten them. Similarly, by de-emphasizing the positive military goal of acquiring additional military facilities for the Soviet Union, Moscow avoids threatening other states in the region that might fear the military strength of the USSR, the USSR's ally, or both. To the extent that Gorbachev can convince non-Marxist Third World governments that the USSR and its allies do not threaten them, he seeks to persuade them that they do not need to rely on the United States for protection.[98]

Gorbachev has gone even further than this. Instead of merely trying to persuade non-Marxist regimes that they do not need U.S. protection, he has tried to convince them that U.S. foreign and military policy seriously threatens their interests.[99] Again, however, Gorbachev appears to recognize that this argument is likely to be persuasive only if the Soviet Union does not undermine it by actively pursuing positive military goals that non-Marxist states regard as threatening.

Gorbachev has sought to achieve negative Soviet military goals in the Third World largely through diplomacy and propaganda. These nonmilitary means, of course, were employed by Gorbachev's predecessors as well. But besides de-emphasizing positive military goals, Gorbachev has modified the Soviet diplomatic and propaganda approach toward non-Marxist states in an attempt to pursue negative military goals more effectively. Most notably, Gorbachev has altered Soviet diplomacy in the area of regional conflict resolution.

Under Gorbachev, Soviet conflict resolution proposals have sought to appeal to all involved parties instead of only those already allied to the USSR. Until Gorbachev came to power, the Soviet Union, as Stephen Sestanovich stated, "has generally been limited to cooperative relations with one side only" in regional conflicts.[100] When the Soviets have tried in the past to mediate conflicts, they have failed to achieve their goal of eliminating U.S. military ties to all states involved. Indeed, the opponent of the state Moscow favored often increased its military reliance on the United States.[101] By appealing to all sides, Gorbachev has attempted to convince all parties in a regional conflict that only the USSR can effect a peaceful resolution to their conflict and to eliminate the incentive for any of the parties to seek an increased U.S. military presence in the region.

These nonmilitary initiatives, of course, are not aimed solely at achieving the negative military goal of reducing U.S. military access to the Third World; they also are intended to address the broader political goal of reducing U.S. influence generally. An analysis of Gorbachev's policy toward different regions of the Third World, however, reveals that he is pursuing specific military objectives in the non-Marxist states of each region. Nevertheless, there are important differences from region to region in the type of military goals Gorbachev is pursuing, the importance that he assigns them, and the means and intensity by which he seeks to achieve them.

Asia and the Pacific

Gorbachev has paid greater attention to Asia and the Pacific as a whole than any of his predecessors. Indeed, he appears to be the first Soviet leader to conceive of Asia and the Pacific as a unified region. He himself has announced a series of initiatives and proposals regarding this region both at Vladivostok in July 1986 and at Krasnoyarsk in September 1988. Several of these initiatives involved China, Japan, Australia, and New Zealand as well as Third World countries. Other proposals were aimed primarily at the Third World countries of the region.

Besides political, diplomatic, and economic goals not discussed here, Gorbachev's policy toward Asia and the Pacific has important military objectives. At Vladivostok, Gorbachev called for (1) "the disbandment of military groups, of the renunciation of foreign bases in Asia and in the Pacific Ocean, and the withdrawal of troops from others' territory"; (2) "an all embracing system of international security" in Asia and the Pacific; (3) nuclear-free zones in Korea, Southeast Asia, and the southern part of the Indian Ocean; (4) "reducing the activity of naval fleets – primarily ships equipped with nuclear arms – in the Pacific Ocean"; (5) limitations on ASW activity in "certain zones" of the Pacific; and (6) discussion of an agreement on the "non-use of violence in the region."[102]

The implementation of these proposals would significantly diminish U.S. military access to Asia and the Pacific. If generally accepted, these proposals would signify that the nations of Asia and the Pacific view the USSR not as a threat but as a protector. Under such a benign security system, there would be no need for any nation to initiate or intensify military relations with the United States. The establishment of such a system would prevent Washington from creating a broader alliance of Pacific nations resembling NATO – a prospect Moscow frequently warns against – and might even lead to the weakening of existing U.S. alliances with the nations of the region. At minimum, as Paul Wolfowitz has observed, "Non-use of force declarations would have no constraining effect on the Soviets. But in more open societies they can influence budgets and force postures."[103]

Moscow has also sought to encourage the nations of the region to seek the removal of U.S. bases and military access to their countries. At Krasnoyarsk, Gorbachev proposed the removal of Soviet naval forces from Cam Ranh Bay in exchange for the closing of U.S. bases in the Philippines.[104] It is doubtful, however, that Gorbachev's offer was serious, given the high value the Soviets place on their military facilities in Vietnam in case of possible conflict with China. In any event, Gorbachev only offered to close one Soviet base in Vietnam in return for the closure of both U.S. bases in the Philippines; he did not offer to withdraw from Soviet military facilities at Da Nang.

Gorbachev may have made the offer anticipating that Washington would immediately reject it – which is what occurred – and that the United States would be blamed locally for the continued militarization of the region. Soviet propaganda under Gorbachev has also actively encouraged the Philippine government – whether led by Ferdinand Marcos or Corazon Aquino – to expel the United States from the Clark and Subic Bay bases.[105]

The Soviets have also sought to promote opposition in the Pacific Island nations to U.S. use of Micronesia for testing ballistic missiles.[106] It would be difficult for the United States to find an alternative testing zone if this campaign were successful. But even if it is unsuccessful, the Soviets hope to arouse fears in the South Pacific that the U.S. testing program as well as the U.S. military presence in the region generally threaten the island nations.

Gorbachev has also expressed support for Indian and Pacific Ocean nuclear-free zones. The Soviets want to deny the United States the ability not only to deploy nuclear weapons targeted against Soviet interests in any country in the region, but also to deploy naval vessels with nuclear weapons in its waters as well. Moscow applauded the 1985 Raratonga treaty establishing a South Pacific nuclear-free zone and, unlike the United States and France, signed two of its protocols. Although not banned by the treaty, the Soviets supported the position of those nations demanding an end to port visits by naval vessels carrying nuclear weapons.[107]

Some analysts have concluded that Soviet fishing

agreements with Kiribati (signed in 1985, lapsed in 1986) and Vanuatu (signed in 1987) are "ill-disguised attempts to gain a strategic foothold" and to obtain military facilities in the South Pacific.[108] This, however, seems unlikely. To begin with, Soviet military facilities in a non-Marxist island nation would only marginally further the USSR's primary military objectives, but would be vulnerable during wartime in a region where the United States and its allies are strong. In addition, the establishment of a Soviet base in this region would probably cause neighboring countries to become fearful of Moscow and seek an increased U.S. military presence. It would undercut Soviet efforts at encouraging South Pacific nations, including Australia and New Zealand, to seek the reduction of America's military presence. A Soviet military presence would also be vulnerable to expulsion by a non-Marxist host government. If Moscow attempted to promote the coming to power of a more pro-Soviet regime, fear of Moscow's intentions would spread generally. It is very likely that the Gorbachev leadership has calculated the costs of pursuing the positive military goal of establishing military facilities in the South Pacific to be far in excess of any possible benefits.

Thus, with the exception of maintaining Soviet military facilities in Vietnam, Gorbachev has basically sought only one military objective in Asia and the Pacific: the negative goal of reducing the U.S. military presence there.

Persian Gulf

Under Gorbachev, the Soviet Union has played a very active military as well as political role in the Persian Gulf region. In the Iran-Iraq war, he has continued his predecessors' policy of providing large-scale direct arms transfers to Baghdad after Iranian forces crossed into Iraqi territory in 1982.[109] Nor has he acted to prevent several of Moscow's allies from selling Soviet weapons to Iran.[110] In 1987, the Soviets leased three oil tankers to Kuwait and sent several naval vessels to protect them against possible Iranian attack.[111] It was the first time the USSR acquired an active role in defending any of the conservative Arab monarchies of the Gulf. Besides these military activities, the Gorbachev leadership actively sought to improve relations with the conservative Arab states as well as Iran while retaining good relations with Iraq.

For the most part, Gorbachev's goals in the Gulf have been political, even though he has pursued them with military means. Generally Moscow has sought to increase its own influence among all countries of the region at the expense of the United States. The Soviets thus have played a delicate game of supporting both the Arabs and the Iranians so that neither feels so threatened by Soviet actions that it seeks (or seeks more) Western support, but instead regards Soviet involvement in the region as desirable. To this end, Moscow claimed that its ability to talk with all sides in the Gulf put the USSR in a better position than the United States to bring about a peaceful resolution to the Iran-Iraq war, given Washington's history of extremely difficult and often hostile relations with Tehran.[112]

The Soviets have contributed to the defense of Iraq to preserve a pro-Soviet regime there and to prevent Iranian influence from expanding in the region generally. The Ba'th regime, however, has not been pro-Soviet enough to allow Moscow to use Iraq for any major military purpose. The most that Moscow can probably hope for from Baghdad after the war is that Iraq will once again allow the Soviet Navy to make use of its port facilities – a privilege cut off at the beginning of the war when the Iranians sealed off the short Iraqi coastline. It is doubtful that this has been a major Soviet military goal during the Iran-Iraq war.

Nevertheless, Gorbachev's policy toward the Gulf indicates that he has specific military objectives in the region. Following Kuwait's invitation to protect some of its oil shipping, Gorbachev has presided over the largest Soviet naval buildup in the Gulf ever, which suggests that Gorbachev was pursuing the positive military goal of acquiring increased military access and perhaps even military facilities in this vital region. The Soviets may have pursued this goal. They may have hoped during the spring and summer of 1987 that the U.S. media, public, and Congress would object to an increased U.S. naval presence in a hostile area, thus forcing Washington to withdraw or scale down its forces. Such a development could have helped the Soviets convince the conservative Arab states that the USSR was their only reliable superpower protector.

Nevertheless, when it became clear by the summer of 1987 that the United States was not going to withdraw to avoid confrontations with Iran but was building up the U.S. naval presence instead, Moscow did not attempt to compete with Washington by further increasing its presence in the Gulf. Instead, Moscow announced that it would not increase the number of its naval vessels there.[113] Perhaps Moscow did not want to distract Iran from its growing hostility to the increased U.S. presence. Indeed, as U.S.-Iranian relations became increasingly confrontational over the summer of 1987, Moscow improved its relations with Tehran.[114]

By the fall of 1987, however, the Soviets were issuing proposals for the withdrawal of all foreign fleets (including their own) from the Gulf and for the creation of a United Nations (UN) fleet. The Soviets also linked their assent to the proposed UN Security Council resolution imposing an arms embargo on Iran to the acceptance of their proposal for a UN fleet to enforce it.[115] In other words, Gorbachev was willing to pay the price of withdrawing the Soviet fleet from the Gulf if withdrawal would mean the removal of the much larger U.S. fleet.

For Gorbachev, then, removing U.S. forces from the Gulf was a more important goal than retaining Soviet forces there. Gorbachev valued the achievement of negative military goals in this region more highly than the achievement of positive ones. To the extent that Gorbachev did pursue positive military goals in the Gulf, he did so at the invitation of one of the conservative monarchies of the Gulf

Cooperation Council and not in opposition to this important group of non-Marxist states.

Although Gorbachev made some progress toward the positive military goal of increasing Soviet naval access to the Gulf, he has so far completely failed to achieve the negative goal of eliminating or even reducing the U.S. and Western naval presence there. Indeed, that presence greatly expanded in 1987. As one Soviet commentator noted, three to five Soviet warships have escorted the three Soviet tankers leased by Kuwait, while by early 1988 the United States had 29 warships and 14 auxiliaries in or near the Gulf.[116] As in the past, Soviet efforts to pursue a positive military goal in this instance contributed to their failure to achieve a negative one.

The Middle East

Gorbachev has modified Soviet policy toward the Arab-Israeli conflict in several ways. He has de-emphasized Soviet support for the hard-line position of Syria and has cut back on Soviet arms transfers to Damascus. At the same time, he has improved Soviet relations with Israel and has decreased Soviet hostility toward the Jewish state generally. In addition, Gorbachev has renewed Soviet calls for a comprehensive Middle East peace conference; he has emphasized that Moscow would seek an agreement that protects both Israeli and Arab interests.[117]

Gorbachev's primary objectives in this region appear to be political rather than military. By de-emphasizing support to Syria, Gorbachev is limiting Damascus's ability to launch another war that could not only complicate U.S.-Soviet relations, but could lead to increased U.S. involvement in the region. By issuing peace proposals designed to be more attractive to moderate Arabs and even to Israelis (to those in the Labor Party anyway), Gorbachev may hope that all parties to the conflict will consider the USSR better able to negotiate peace in the region than the United States, given poor U.S. relations with Syria.

The Gorbachev leadership, however, appears to calculate that to the extent Moscow is successful in achieving these political goals, it will be better able to achieve its negative military goals. The Soviets may hope that because they have reduced their military assistance to Damascus, the moderate Arab states and even Israel will consider the USSR and Syria as less of a threat. Moderate Arabs might then see no need to increase their military ties to Washington and perhaps might even reduce them because of unhappiness over U.S. support to Israel. Gorbachev seems to be devoting considerable effort to cultivating Egypt. It is doubtful that Cairo would allow the Soviets to renew their military presence there, but Gorbachev may not be seeking this goal at present. The Soviets, however, have been encouraging Cairo to reduce the U.S. military presence in Egypt.[118] This is probably Gorbachev's most important negative military goal in the region.

Nevertheless, Gorbachev has not given up all positive military goals in this area. In August 1988, U.S. government sources revealed that the Soviets were expanding their military facilities at Tartūs on the coast of Syria. This move appears designed more to strengthen the Soviet position in the Mediterranean generally than in the region of the Arab-Israeli conflict specifically. As one observer noted, Tartūs is currently "the Soviets' only operating naval base in the Mediterranean." The expansion of this facility will mean that Soviet naval vessels will not have to return as often to home ports in the Black, Baltic, and Barents seas and will thus allow the Soviets to keep surface ships and submarines on station in the Mediterranean longer.[119]

Gorbachev may hope that pursuit of this one positive military goal in the region will not harm pursuit of the negative military goal and overall political objective of reducing U.S. influence. Neither Israel nor even the moderate Arab states, however, are going to regard the expanded Soviet base at Tartūs as something that does not threaten their interests, especially if it becomes apparent that Syria's price for allowing such expansion is increased Soviet arms transfers of sophisticated weapons to Damascus.

Africa

In Africa as well, Gorbachev has de-emphasized the giving of military support to Marxist and radical non-Marxist states in their disputes with neighboring pro-Western states (he has, however, continued significant military aid to help Marxist states defeat their internal opponents). Instead, Gorbachev has encouraged – and in some instances actively worked to bring about – political solutions to interstate conflicts between pro-Soviet states on the one hand and their pro-Western neighbors on the other.

Gorbachev did almost nothing to help defend Libya against U.S. raids in March and April of 1986. On the second occasion, Soviet naval vessels off Tripoli reportedly received advance notice of the approaching U.S. aircraft and pulled out to sea without warning the Libyans of the impending attack. It is, of course, understandable that the Soviets wanted to avoid involvement in the U.S.-Libyan confrontation. Moscow has traditionally sought to avoid situations where there was a risk of a direct clash and escalating conflict with Washington. But Gorbachev did not give Qadhafi significant military aid during 1987 to prevent the French-backed forces of Chad's President Hissein Habré from driving the Libyans out of northern Chad (which they had occupied for several years).[120] The Soviets apparently did not want fear of Libyan expansionism to make Libya's neighbors afraid of both Tripoli and Moscow and thus more desirous of an increased Western military presence to defend themselves.

In the Horn of Africa, the Soviets under Gorbachev have frequently called for a peaceful resolution to the Somali-Ethiopian conflict. An agreement was reached in the spring of 1988 whereby the two sides agreed not to fight over the border and not to give military assistance to the other side's internal opponents. In this case, the political resolution of a conflict with a neighbor helps Ethiopia's efforts to defeat its internal opponents. At the same time, it serves to reduce tensions and decrease the incentive for Somalia to seek a greater U.S. military presence in the region. In fact, because Somalia faces a serious insurgency, it has an interest in maintaining good relations with Moscow so that the Kremlin will restrain Ethiopia from supporting its internal opponents.[121]

Again, Gorbachev's primary aims in Africa are political. By discouraging Moscow's Marxist and radical non-Marxist allies from undertaking hostile actions against other non-Marxist states and by encouraging peaceful resolution of conflicts instead, the Soviets hope to increase their own influence in Africa while eliminating opportunities for U.S. influence to increase. In the military realm, Gorbachev is not attempting to achieve additional positive military goals by increasing Soviet military access to additional non-Marxist states (though he apparently seeks to retain limited military access to Libya). Instead, the Soviets appear to be concentrating on the negative military goal of preventing the United States from gaining military access to additional countries in Africa and even reducing U.S. access to those countries where it has military facilities.

Latin America

The Soviets under Gorbachev have launched a major effort to improve Moscow's relations with almost all of the non-Marxist states of Latin America (there are exceptions such as Chile, Paraguay, and El Salvador). The pursuit of military goals is not a major thrust of Soviet policy toward this region that is so far away from the USSR. The Soviets are not attempting to achieve positive military goals with regard to the non-Marxist states of the region. Although Moscow may wish to preserve and even enhance its military access to Cuba and Nicaragua, it is not attempting to ac-

quire facilities in other Latin nations. The Soviets are, however, pursuing negative military goals in this region to some
extent. As noted earlier, the Soviets are encouraging Panamanian strongman Manuel Noriega's opposition to U.S. efforts to depose him and restore republican democracy. Moscow's ultimate aim may be the denial of U.S. military access
to Panama as well as preferential U.S. access to the Canal.
Nevertheless, this goal is unlikely to be achieved before the
expiration of the treaty that provides for complete Panamanian control of the Canal Zone in 1999 (if then).

Soviet diplomacy and propaganda has focused on convincing the governments and people of the major non-
Marxist states of Latin America that the Sandinista regime
and its ties to the USSR are not a threat to them. Instead,
the Soviets seek to convince other Latin American nations
that Nicaragua is a normal state like them and that U.S.
hostility directed now at Nicaragua may in future be directed at them. Although Moscow does not expect Latin American states to seek Soviet military help in defending themselves against the United States – such a Soviet connection
might lead to increased U.S. hostility – the Soviets do seem
to hope that Latin Americans generally will consider the
United States more of a threat than the USSR. Moscow does
not want Latin Americans to perceive Soviet support for Nicaragua as a reason for them to fear the USSR and thus seek a
greater U.S. military presence for their protection.[122]

Conclusion

Gorbachev has reoriented Soviet military policy away from
supporting Marxist and radical non-Marxist states against
more moderate pro-U.S. ones. Gorbachev's minimum goal is
the same as his predecessors' – to persuade moderate and
conservative Third World states to think of the USSR not
as an enemy but as a friend, thus reducing their motivation
to increase military cooperation with the West. Beyond

this, Gorbachev (also like his predecessors) seeks to convince moderate Third World governments that the United States threatens their interests and that they should therefore work with Moscow to diminish or eliminate the U.S. presence in their country or region.

Yet if moderate Third World governments (or immoderate but not pro-Soviet ones such as Iran) accept the former or even the latter Soviet argument, it is highly unlikely that they will grant military facilities to the USSR or allow a large Communist military presence in their countries. Although this military presence was the ultimate goal of Soviet military policy toward non-Marxist states before Gorbachev, the new Soviet leader has de-emphasized this goal dramatically; he has not eliminated it completely, however. For him, it is less important if non-Marxist Third World states do not become firm Soviet allies. Past experience has shown that when one does, one or more neighboring states turn closer to the United States – which is exactly what Gorbachev wants to avoid. Besides, the USSR already possesses a significant base structure in certain Marxist Third World states that Gorbachev can be relatively confident he will retain. He seeks instead to improve relations with as many non-Marxist states as possible in a way that other such states will not consider threatening. His objective, then, is not to increase the USSR's military alliances with these states but to create such conditions that these states will diminish or even end their military alliances with the West. Although this Soviet policy is not a purely military one because it involves important diplomatic and propaganda components, its success could have important implications for the overall U.S.-Soviet military balance.

Although Gorbachev has indeed made some progress in improving Soviet relations – including military ones – with several important non-Marxist Third World states, he has so far failed to persuade non-Marxist Third World states (besides the ones Moscow was already closely allied with) to diminish significantly their military relations with the

West. Nevertheless, because the policy is long term, it may yield benefits for Moscow. In the meantime it avoids many of the problems caused by Moscow's pre-Gorbachev policy of allying primarily with Marxist and radical non-Marxist states.

6

Gorbachev, the Third World, and the Future

Far from abandoning the Third World, Soviet military policy under Gorbachev seeks to strengthen Moscow's (and weaken Washington's) position in Asia, Africa, and Latin America. This goal, of course, was sought by Gorbachev's predecessors as well. But Gorbachev has significantly changed the way current Soviet military policy pursues this goal as opposed to the way Brezhnev did.

Brezhnev's military policy toward the Third World in the 1970s assumed that U.S. power was waning. Brezhnev appeared to conclude that the United States was not only unable to prevent increased Soviet military involvement in the Third World, but also could not afford to make an issue of it because it would jeopardize arms control agreements that the United States was believed to want more than the USSR. Brezhnev also assumed that Marxist revolution was the wave of the future and that the USSR and its allies could help Marxist regimes arise or consolidate power quickly and cheaply. As a result, military involvement in the Third World could hardly be a great burden to the Soviet economy. Brezhnev, then, regarded the pursuit of positive military objectives in the Third World as a low-cost, high-yield endeavor.

Gorbachev recognized that these assumptions were incorrect. In the 1980s, U.S. power was rising, not falling. The U.S. Senate's refusal to ratify the SALT II treaty after the Soviet invasion of Afghanistan proved that the United States was not so desirous of arms control that it would overlook any Soviet intervention in the Third World. Gorbachev also saw that intervention in the Third World did not lead to quick, easy victories, but costly involvements to support weak Marxist allies in seemingly interminable conflicts. Because he regarded finding the resources to modernize and restructure the Soviet economy as urgently necessary, he saw costly Soviet efforts to prop up weak Marxist regimes as harmful to his domestic priorities. Furthermore, to achieve his domestic priorities, Gorbachev required détente and arms control with the United States. Finally, Gorbachev appeared to recognize that Marxist revolution was unlikely to spread to the most important Third World states and that a Soviet military policy that supported primarily Marxist and radical non-Marxist regimes risked alienating the most important moderate states.

Gorbachev has modified and subordinated Soviet military policy toward the Third World to support his more important goals of reforming the Soviet economy and achieving arms control agreements with the United States (without which an arms race preventing the implementation of perestroika could occur). Thus, Gorbachev has decreased Soviet support to Marxist revolution, drastically reduced the Soviet military effort to defend the weak Marxist regime in Afghanistan, de-emphasized support to radical non-Marxist states, and increased efforts to achieve conflict resolution agreements. Gorbachev, then, apparently regards the pursuit of positive military goals in the Third World as a high-cost, low-yield endeavor.

These changes Gorbachev has made in Soviet military policy are designed not only to serve his higher priority internal and external goals, but also to enhance Soviet ability to pursue negative military goals in the Third World. Gorbachev seeks to capitalize on his de-emphasis on positive military goals in the Third World to eliminate any incentive for non-Marxist states—especially the most important ones—to cooperate with the West militarily against Soviet interests.

Gorbachev's military policy toward the Third World is certainly more cautious and pessimistic than was Brezhnev's. Nevertheless, if successful, this more cautious and pessimistic military policy would result in a significantly weakened U.S. military position in the Third World. Decreased U.S. military access to non-Marxist states would hinder U.S. ability to harm Soviet interests and protect its own. In addition, the United States is a major maritime power dependent on access to overseas facilities. Increased unwillingness on the part of non-Marxist Third World states to cooperate militarily with Washington could lead to mounting hostility between the United States and its traditional Third World allies. Such a development, of course, would serve Soviet interests.

Nevertheless, Gorbachev faces important problems in attempting to reduce U.S. military access to the Third World. One problem is that of persuading moderate non-Marxist Third World states that the USSR does not threaten their security whereas the United States threatens it so much that they should reduce their U.S. military ties. Many moderate governments remain fearful of the Soviet Union because of its previous support for revolution against them or their neighbors, or its support for the neighboring Marxist or radical non-Marxist regimes that had threatened them. They fear that although the Soviets are now de-emphasizing support for revolution, this policy could change in the future.

Even if Moscow manages to convince moderate non-Marxist states that the USSR is no longer a revolutionary power and that there is no need to cooperate with the United States militarily, long-term Soviet success in reducing or eliminating Third World military cooperation with the United States depends on the long-term continuation of nonthreatening Soviet behavior toward moderate Third World states. It is insufficient for Moscow to convince such governments on one occasion that the USSR is their friend (while the United States is not) and then expect to prevent their allying with the United States forever. Furthermore, moderate non-Marxist states are highly unlikely to allow the USSR and its allies to achieve so strong a position internally that Moscow could prevent realliance with the West as the Soviets have done in several Marxist states. Indeed, even the attempt to gain influence over a non-Marxist state's policy-making process could lead that state and others to fear the USSR and seek U.S. protection.

Of course, if Gorbachev were ousted by his hard-line rivals, the latter might consciously jettison his entire strategy of appealing to moderate non-Marxist states and instead re-emphasize Marxist and radical non-Marxist regimes. As under Brezhnev, however, this course would probably turn moderate non-Marxist states all the more closely to the West and allow the USSR to retain as allies only a few Marxist and radical non-Marxist allies involved in perpetual conflict. Even if Soviet conservatives came to power but tried very hard to continue Gorbachev's policy of befriending moderate non-Marxist governments, their efforts might fail if they also increased political and military support to Moscow's Marxist and radical non-Marxist allies.

It seems highly unlikely, however, that Gorbachev will be ousted in the near future. At the end of September 1988, he strengthened his position by restructuring the party and the government apparatus, as well as by weakening or purging many of his opponents. Now more than ever, Gorbachev is unlikely to actively pursue positive military goals because this would harm his efforts to achieve other goals, including negative military ones, in the Third World. Even so, he might still find it difficult to persuade moderate non-Marxist governments to end military cooperation with Washington and limit U.S. access to their countries and regions for three reasons:

1. As occurred in the past, pro-Soviet Marxist or other revolutionaries could come to power without much or any Soviet support. But neighboring countries and the United

States might perceive that the USSR was involved, especially if the new regime feels vulnerable and requests Soviet military assistance.

2. Outright or potential conflicts between Third World nations are likely to persist well into the future. Gorbachev has made increased efforts to work with all sides to mediate several of these interstate conflicts, but so far has had only modest success. In any given conflict, as long as one side is firmly allied to the United States, one side is firmly allied to the USSR, or one side refuses to negotiate whether or not it is allied to either superpower, Gorbachev will find it difficult to bring about an end to the conflict or to exclude U.S. involvement.

3. Even if the most important non-Marxist Third World states improve their relations with the Soviet Union, it is highly doubtful that many of them would seek to support the Soviet goal of excluding U.S. military access to their region entirely. Many of them have important economic relations with the West — far more important than their economic relations with the Soviet bloc — which they would not want to risk disrupting. More important, non-Marxist states might consider improved relations with the USSR a means to increase their independence and maneuverability vis-à-vis both superpowers. But working with Moscow to exclude U.S. access would hinder, not help, the achievement of this goal. Finally, certain large non-Marxist states (such as India and Iran) that do wish to diminish the U.S. military presence in their regions do not want an increased Soviet military presence there either. They want the USSR merely to support their own great power ambitions, not to compete with them.

Thus, even if Gorbachev's military policy toward the Third World is strictly unrevolutionary and a model of restraint, within the Third World there are serious obstacles to achieving the negative military goal of diminishing U.S. military access to Asia, Africa, and Latin America as well as to the oceans and seas surrounding them — obstacles that are not easily overcome.

Notes

1. Adam B. Ulam, *Expansion and Coexistence: Soviet Foreign Policy 1917-73*, 2nd ed. (New York: Praeger, 1974), 167–183, and Richard Lowenthal, *Model or Ally? The Communist Powers and the Developing Countries* (New York: Oxford University Press, 1977), 184–185.

2. For an excellent account of Soviet efforts to acquire naval facilities, based on negotiating records in the Egyptian naval archives, see Mohrez M. El Hussini, *Soviet-Egyptian Relations, 1945-85* (London: Macmillan, 1987).

3. On Soviet actions in Cuba in 1962, see Herbert S. Dinerstein, *The Making of a Missile Crisis: October 1962* (Baltimore: Johns Hopkins University Press, 1976).

4. Mark N. Katz, *The Third World in Soviet Military Thought* (Baltimore: Johns Hopkins University Press, 1982), 18–20.

5. There have been a number of excellent works on Soviet policy toward the Third World under Khrushchev and Brezhnev. Among others, see Stephen T. Hosmer and Thomas W. Wolfe, *Soviet Policy and Practice toward Third World Conflicts* (Lexington, Ma.: Lexington, 1983); Bruce D. Porter, *The USSR in Third World Conflicts* (Cambridge: Cambridge University Press, 1984); and Joseph G. Whelan and Michael J. Dixon, *The Soviet Union in the Third World: Threat to World Peace?* (Washington, D.C.: Pergamon-Brassey's, 1986).

6. See Michael MccGwire, *Military Objectives in Soviet For-*

eign Policy (Washington, D.C.: The Brookings Institution, 1987).

7. Stephen Sestanovich, "Do the Soviets Feel Pinched by Third World Adventures?" *The Washington Post*, May 20, 1984.

8. Prof. Vyacheslav Dashichev, "East-West: Quest for New Relations. On the Priorities of the Soviet State's Foreign Policy," *Literaturnaya Gazeta*, May 18, 1988, p. 14 in *FBIS-SOV*, May 20, 1988, pp. 4–8.

9. Gorbachev's policy toward Cambodia and Angola will be discussed more fully in chapter 4.

10. Gorbachev's policy toward revolutionary movements will be examined in detail in chapter 3.

11. Michael R. Gordon, "Soviets Scale Back Naval Deployments and Large Exercises," *New York Times*, July 17, 1988.

12. Ibid.

13. Colonel V. Larionov, "Politicheskaya storona sovetskoy voyennoy doktrina," *Kommunist Vooruzhennykh Sil*, no. 22 (November 1968), 16. During the Khrushchev era, a senior Soviet military thinker wrote, "In recent times in the imperialist camp, much has been said not only of local wars, but of the formation of special forces to be employed in such wars. A special theory of brushfire wars has been elaborated. In actuality, such wars cannot remain local for long: they contain a threat for all humanity. A small imperialist war, as N. S. Khrushchev has noted, regardless of which of the imperialists started it, can develop into a world war." Colonel General N. Lomov, "O sovetskoy voyennoy doktrine," *Kommunist Vooruzhennykh Sil*, no. 10 (May 1962), 16.

14. Colonel G. Malinovskiy, "Lokal'niye voini v zone natsional'no-osvoboditel'nogo dvizheniya," *Voyenno-istoricheskiy Zhurnal*, no. 5 (May 1974), 97. In 1975, the then commandant of the General Staff Academy also wrote that local war could be kept localized: "In terms of scope and weapons employed, a local war [lokal'naya voina] is a local [mestnaya], small war. In comparison to world war, it can be limited by the number of participant countries and the limits of a defined geographic region of military actions and, as a rule, is waged with conventional weapons." General of the Army I. Shavrov, "Lokal'niye voini i ikh mesto v globalnoy strategii imperializma" (part 1), ibid., no. 3 (March 1975), 61.

15. Francis Fukuyama, *Soviet Civil-Military Relations and the Power Projection Mission*, R-35-4-AF (Santa Monica, Ca.: Rand Corp., April 1987), 17–29.

16. See Katz, *The Third World in Soviet Military Thought*, chap. 3.

17. Fukuyama, *Soviet Civil-Military Relations and the Power Projection Mission*, chap. 4.

18. See, for example, Colonel General G. Dol'nikov, "Razvitiye taktiki aviatsii v lokal'nykh voinakh," *Voyenno-istoricheskiy Zhurnal*, no. 12 (December 1983), 34–43; Major General M. Fesenko, "Ognevoye porazheniye nazemnykh sredstv PVO," ibid., no. 5 (May 1984), 66–73; Major General V. Maksimov, "Udary po aerodroman," ibid., no. 6 (June 1984), 79–84; Colonel R. Loskutov and Colonel V. Morozov, "Nekotorye voprosy taktiki vooruzhennogo konflikta v Livane v 1982 godu," ibid., no. 7 (July 1984), 75–80; Admiral P. Navoitsev, "Deistviya VMS protiv berega," ibid., no. 8 (August 1984), 47–52; and Colonel V. Odintsov, "Tylovoye obespecheniye voisk s primeneniem aviatsii po opytu lokal'nykh voin," ibid., no. 2 (February 1985), 81–86.

19. A. I. Zevelev, Yu. A. Polyakov, and A. I. Chugunov, *Basmachestvo: Vozniknoveniye, sushchnost', krakh* (Moscow: Nauka, 1981), 6; and B. Lunin, ed., *Basmachestvo: Sotsial'no-politicheskaya sushchnost'* (Tashkent: Iz. "Fan" Uzbekskoy SSR, 1984), 3.

20. B. V. Panov, ed., *Istoriya voennogo iskusstva* (Moscow: Voenizdat, 1984), 503–504. See also, General of the Army I. E. Shavrov, *Lokal'nye voyny: Istoriya i sovremennost'* (Moscow: Voenizdat, 1981).

21. P. A. Zhilin, ed., *Istoriya voennogo iskusstva* (Moscow: Voenizdat, 1986).

22. N. Yefimov, "Revolyutsionnyy protsess i sovremennost'," *Kommunist Vorruzhennykh Sil*, no. 7 (April 1987), 86. See also, A. A. Migolat'ev, *Imperializm: stavka na voynu* (Moscow: Voenizdat, 1985), 57; and I. Nechaev, "NATO – v pogone za voennym prevoskhodstvom," *Mezhdunarodnaya Zhizn*, no. 4 (April 1987), 64–65.

23. For a statement accusing the Reagan administration of preparing for "fighting a protracted general war with the use of conventional means of destruction against the USSR and its allies simultaneously in several theaters of war and theaters of military action," see R. G. Simonyan, *Real'naya opasnost': voennye bloki imperializma* (Moscow: Voenizdat, 1985), 63.

24. This article strongly advocates pursuit of détente and avoidance of military involvement in the Third World. A. V.

Kozyrev (deputy chief of the International Organizations Administration, USSR Ministry of Foreign Affairs), "Confidence and the Balance of Interests," *Mezhdunarodnaya Zhizn*, no. 10 (October 1988), 3–12.

25. See, for example, the statements made by Marshal Sergei Akhromeyev (Belgrade Tanjug in English, January 16, 1988 in *FBIS-SOV*, January 19, 1988, p. 18; and Moscow International Service in Czech, May 6, 1988 in *FBIS-SOV*, May 10, 1988, p. 75), Defense Minister Dimitri Yazov ("Feat for the Sake of Life," *Pravda*, May 9, 1988, p. 2 in *FBIS-SOV*, May 10, 1988, p. 71); and the commander of Soviet forces in Afghanistan, Lt. General Boris Gromov (Moscow TASS in English, May 14, 1988 in *FBIS-SOV*, May 16, 1988, pp. 25–26; and at his speech to the 19th Party Conference, *Pravda*, July 2, 1988, p. 7 in *FBIS-SOV*, July 6, 1988, p. 19).

26. See in particular Lyudmila Shchipakhina, "Motherland Is Welcoming Its Sons," *Krasnaya Zvezda*, May 22, 1988, p. 2 in *FBIS-SOV*, May 24, 1988, pp. 33–34: "I think about whether anyone is to blame for everything which has happened in Afghanistan and which has affected us so painfully. Our conscience as Communists would never have allowed us not to respond to the call of a revolutionary government. Our peace policy and our friendly relations with the fraternal countries also obliged us to respond to the call for help. But the real conditions of aid and the internal situation in Afghanistan proved far more complex than this broad and friendly impulse. I think that the Afghan comrades, the fighters for the April revolution at its various levels, have not done everything possible to exert subtle and balanced influence on people's consciousness, attracting them to their side. In some places and in some respects the ideas of the April revolution have not reached the consciousness of a people of many tribes, a society of many strata. The frenzied fanaticism of the opponents of the revolution and the traditions of inflexibility and bellicosity inherent in the Afghans were not considered.

"Afghanistan will be the way the Afghans want to see it. The people must choose their path of development for themselves."

27. Aleksandr Prokhanov, "Afghan Questions," *Literaturnaya Gazeta*, February 17, 1988, pp. 1, 9, in *FBIS-SOV*, February 18, 1988, pp. 32–34; Lt. Col. A. Oliynik, "We Believe in a Peaceful Life," *Krasnaya Zvezda*, April 16, 1988, p. 5 in *FBIS-SOV*, April

22, 1988, p. 22; and interview with Colonel General V. Lomov, Moscow TASS in English, May 11, 1988 in *FBIS-SOV*, May 11, 1988, p. 16.

28. A. Gorokhov, B. Kotov, and V. Okulov, "Days of Hope and Anxiety," *Pravda*, May 15, 1988, pp. 1, 6, in *FBIS-SOV*, May 17, 1988, pp. 30–33.

29. According to General Lizichev, "The withdrawal time-table has been well thought-out and supported. Those who try to wreck it will be most resolutely crushed." Capt. 2nd Rank V. Kocherov, "Afghanistan: Observe the Geneva Agreements," *Krasnaya Zvezda*, May 26, 1988, p. 4 in *FBIS-SOV*, May 26, 1988, p. 26. See also, Paris AFP in English, May 25, 1988 in *FBIS-SOV*, May 25, 1988, p. 28.

30. Najibullah stated, "At present the defense ministries of the Republic of Afghanistan and the USSR are deciding on the precise number of advisers which can be maintained in the future, too. I know that this will be a minimum number in the top echelon and several dozen Soviet instructors in our military training establishments." Najibullah press conference, Moscow International Service in Russian, April 28, 1988 in *FBIS-SOV*, April 29, 1988, pp. 20–21.

31. Press conference with Lt. General Boris Gromov, Moscow TASS in English, May 14, 1988 in *FBIS-SOV*, May 16, 1988, p. 25.

32. D. T. Yazov, "Feat for the Sake of Life," *Pravda*, May 9, 1988, p. 2 in *FBIS-SOV*, May 10, 1988, p. 71; and East Berlin, *Neues Deutschland*, May 12, 1988, pp. 3, 4, in *FBIS-SOV*, May 17, 1988, p. 46.

33. Philip Taubman, "Moscow Suspends Pullout of Its Afghanistan Forces; Charges Violations of Pact," *New York Times*, November 5, 1988.

34. David B. Ottaway, "U.S. Concerned about Soviets' Use of Bombers in Afghanistan," *Washington Post*, November 1, 1988; and Robert Pear, "Soviets Said to Deploy Missiles in Kabul," *New York Times*, November 2, 1988.

35. N. Shapalin, "Patrioty, internatsionalisty," *Krasnaya Zvezda*, April 3, 1987, pp. 2–3.

36. Moscow TV Service in Russian, January 16, 1988 in *FBIS-SOV*, January 22, 1988, p. 65. In September 1987 a Soviet air force general warned that political means for resolving conflicts had to be supported by military means: "The comprehen-

sive combination of political and military means to defend revolutionary achievements is also expressed in the national conciliation in Afghanistan, Kampuchea and other countries. The strengthened defenses of those countries and the decisive repelling of military attacks by counterrevolutionaries who are incited by the West support the primary purpose – using primarily political means to halt the bloody undeclared war of imperialism and its minions."

He further stated: "The lesson of 1941 teaches us how important it is to flexibly and harmoniously combine political and military methods to defend socialism without reducing the role of a strong and invincible defense. In addition, history provides many other examples where aggressors used negotiations and even 'adjustments' to relationships to weaken the vigilance of future enemies." Lt. General of Aviation V. Serebryannikov, "Correlating the Political and Military Methods in the Defense of Socialism," *Kommunist Vooruzhennykh Sil*, no. 18 (September 1987), 9–16 in Joint Publications Research Service, *Soviet Union: Military Affairs* (JPRS-UMA-87-045 – December 23, 1987), 17.

37. Moscow TASS in English, August 5, 1988 in *FBIS-SOV*, August 5, 1988, p. 33. This speech may have been made in reaction to Foreign Minister Shevardnadze's statement at the Party Conference that peaceful coexistence took precedence over the struggle against capitalism. See "Behind the Master's Back," *The Economist*, August 20, 1988, p. 39.

38. On Stalin's support for revolution in the Third World, see Ulam, *Expansion and Coexistence*, 111–125, 167–183, and Richard Lowenthal, *Model or Ally? The Communist Powers and the Developing Countries* (New York: Oxford University Press, 1977), 184–185.

39. For an excellent article discussing the alternating periods of strong and weak Soviet support to revolution, see Francis Fukuyama, "Patterns of Soviet Third World Policy," *Problems of Communism* 36, no. 5 (September–October 1987): 1–13; see also Ulam, *Expansion and Coexistence*, 167–183.

40. Stephen T. Hosmer and Thomas W. Wolfe, *Soviet Policy and Practice toward Third World Conflicts* (Lexington, Ma.: Lexington/D. C. Heath, 1983), chaps. 2–4, and Katz, *The Third World in Soviet Military Thought*, 16–34.

41. For an excellent analysis of Moscow's aid to Third World revolutionary groups, see Galia Golan, *The Soviet Union and Na-*

tional Liberation Movements in the Third World (Boston: Unwin Hyman, 1988), chap. 6. See also Hosmer and Wolfe, *Soviet Policy and Practice toward Third World Conflicts*, chaps. 5–7, and Katz, *The Third World in Soviet Military Thought*, chaps. 2–4.

42. The increased pessimism about the prospects for Marxism in the Third World among Soviet academic specialists preceded Gorbachev's rise to power. For a provocative analysis of this trend, see Jerry Hough, *The Struggle for the Third World* (Washington, D.C.: The Brookings Institution, 1986). For a recent Soviet statement indicating greatly diminished expectations for revolution in the Third World, see A. V. Kozyrev, "Confidence and the Balance of Interests," *Mezhdunarodnaya Zhizn*, no. 10 (October 1988), 3–12.

43. See, for example, Gorbachev's speech at the 27th Party Congress: Moscow TV Service in Russian, February 25, 1986 in *FBIS-SOV*, February 26, 1986, pp. 7–8, 28–34.

44. Moscow TV Service in Russian, November 2, 1987 in *FBIS-SOV*, November 3, 1987, p. 58.

45. Mark N. Katz, *Russia and Arabia: Soviet Foreign Policy toward the Arabian Peninsula* (Baltimore: Johns Hopkins University Press, 1986), 108–119, and idem, "Soviet Policy in the Middle East," *Current History* 87 (February 1988), 58.

46. David Rosenberg, "Communism in the Philippines," *Problems of Communism* 33, no. 5 (September–October 1984): 29–34, and Gareth Porter, "Philippine Communism after Marcos," *Problems of Communism* 36, no. 5 (September–October 1987): 14–35. Moscow did not support the NPA insurgency in the 1970s either, but it was much weaker then. Much has been made of the fact that the NPA is "Maoist" and thus anti-Soviet. But to the extent that the NPA is pro-Chinese, it espouses the Maoism of twenty years ago and has little in common with the Chinese government of today. The NPA apparently receives no aid from Beijing. To the extent that it is anti-Soviet, the NPA may only be so because the Soviets have not given it any military assistance. This might well change if Moscow was willing to do so.

47. See, for example, Moscow TASS in English, February 4, 1986 in *FBIS-SOV*, February 5, 1986, p. A8; and N. Alexeyev, "Preelection Steam," *New Times*, no. 5 (February 1986): 14–15.

48. Among many others, see Moscow Domestic Service in Russian, April 4, 1988 in *FBIS-SOV*, April 4, 1988, p. 28; and

G. Zafesov, "There Will Not Be Any Laurels," *Pravda*, April 21, 1988, p. 5 in *FBIS-SOV*, April 25, 1988, pp. 57–58.

49. Ilya Prizel, "Latin America: The Long March," *The National Interest*, no. 12 (Summer 1988): 117–119.

For Soviet commentary that portrays non-Marxist Central American governments as "U.S. imperialism's" victims and not collaborators, see Vladimir Dolgov, "The Troubles of the 'Rich Coast,'" *New Times*, no. 35 (September 1986): 28–30; and R. Padilla Rush, "Honduras: A Focal Point of Confrontation with Imperialism," *World Marxist Review*, no. 12 (December 1986): 23–29.

50. The most far-reaching of these statements have not appeared in the Soviet press, but have been made by African specialists Viktor Goncharev and Gleb Starushenko as well as other Soviets to foreign journalists or scholars. See "'Glasnost' on Southern Africa," *Front File: Southern Africa*, no. 3 (July 1987): 1–3; "Meet Mikhail Gorbachev's Pariah Diplomacy," *The Economist*, May 28, 1988, pp. 39–40; Allister Sparks, "Moscow's New Game in Africa," *Washington Post* (Outlook), October 9, 1988; and John F. Burns, "Soviets, in Shift, Press for Accord in South Africa," *New York Times*, March 16, 1989.

51. "Meet Mikhail Gorbachev's Pariah Diplomacy," 39–40.

52. Moscow in Spanish to Chile, November 19, 1985 in *FBIS-SOV*, November 25, 1985, pp. K2–3; Moscow in Spanish to Chile, November 20, 1986 in *FBIS-SOV*, December 5, 1986, pp. K1–2; and Moscow TASS in English, December 22, 1987 in *FBIS-SOV*, December 23, 1987, p. 22.

53. Moscow Radio Peace and Progress in Spanish to Latin America, May 12, 1986 in *FBIS-SOV*, May 15, 1986, p. K2; and Julio Rojas, "Attractive Force of the October Revolution's Ideals and Cause," *World Marxist Review*, no. 11 (November 1986): 9.

54. Moscow TASS in English, April 24, 1986 in *FBIS-SOV*, April 25, 1986, p. K1; Alexander Baryshev, "An Odious Comparison," *New Times*, no. 22 (June 1986), 16–17. See also, Moscow TASS in English, April 10, 1988 in *FBIS-SOV*, April 11, 1988, p. 60, and Prizel, "Latin America: The Long March."

55. Y. Bochkaryov, "Crimes of Apartheid Continue," *New Times*, no. 15 (April 1985): 15; Anatoli Gromyko, "Racism and Colonialism in Africa Must Be Ended!" *Asia and Africa Today*, no. 4 (July–August 1986): 6–8; Moscow in Zulu to Southern Africa, July 27, 1986 in *FBIS-SOV*, August 5, 1986, pp. J1–2; "U.S.A.-

South Africa: The Same Root," *New Times*, no. 35 (September 1986): 7–8; "Apartheid Regime in Deep Crisis," *New Times*, no. 2 (January 1987): 21; and "Africa," *New Times*, no. 5 (February 1987): 8.

56. See, for example, Hosmer and Wolfe, *Soviet Practice toward Third World Conflicts*, 159.

57. Fukuyama, *Soviet Civil-Military Relations and the Power Projection Mission*, 52.

58. U.S. Department of Defense, *Soviet Military Power: An Assessment of the Threat, 1988* (Washington, D.C.: U.S. Government Printing Office, April 1988), 83.

59. Ibid., 138.

60. In its publications on arms transfers, the U.S. Arms Control and Disarmament Agency (ACDA) follows the irritating practice of not publishing annual figures for transfers by the major arms producers to individual countries. Instead, ACDA publishes one table listing the cumulative value of arms transfers for a five-year period by major supplier to recipient country and another table listing total arms transfers to recipient country on an annual basis. For those countries that have received significant arms transfers from several countries over a five-year period, it is impossible to figure out what each supplier gave the recipient in each of the five years. However, for those countries that have received nearly all their arms from one supplier over a five-year period, the figures for the total annual arms transfers to a recipient can be read as figures for the one supplier. The USSR is virtually the exclusive supplier of arms to most Marxist Third World states, including Vietnam and Cambodia.

External sources supplied Vietnam with $1.4 billion worth of arms in 1982, $1.5 billion in 1983, $1.3 billion in 1984, $1.1 billion in 1985, and $1.6 billion in 1986 – virtually all of which came from the USSR and only a very small amount from Poland and others. External sources also provided the Heng Samrin government with $70 million worth of arms in 1982, $140 million in 1983, $190 million in 1984, $280 million in 1985, and $150 million in 1986 – almost all of which came from the USSR. U.S. Arms Control and Disarmament Agency, *World Military Expenditures and Arms Transfers: 1987* (Washington, D.C.: U.S. Government Printing Office, March 1988), 94, 97, 124, 128–129.

In October 1988, then CIA Deputy Director Robert Gates gave speeches at forums sponsored by the American Association for the Advancement of Science and by the U.S. Air Force. According to Gates, the Soviets gave $2 billion in military assistance to Vietnam, Laos, and Cambodia in 1987.

61. See, for example, Moscow TASS in English, March 28, 1985 in *FBIS-SOV*, March 29, 1985, p. E1.

62. Boris Barakhta, "Futile Venture," *Pravda*, March 22, 1986, p. 5 in *FBIS-SOV*, March 28, 1986, p. E3.

63. See B. Vinogradov, "Constructive Approach," *Izvestiya*, August 19, 1985, p. 4 in *FBIS-SOV*, August 22, 1985, pp. E1-2; and "For the Sake of National Accord," *Izvestiya*, September 19, 1985, p. 5 in *FBIS-SOV*, September 25, 1985, p. E3.

64. Moscow TASS in English, May 14, 1987 in *FBIS-SOV*, May 20, 1987, p. E1; Y. Buksin, "We Earned the Right to Live in Peace," *Moscow News*, September 13, 1987, p. 10 in *FBIS-SOV*, September 24, 1987, p. 32; and Soviet Government Statement, Moscow TASS International Service in Russian, October 17, 1987 in *FBIS-SOV*, October 20, 1987, pp. 32-33.

65. Gorbachev speech, *Pravda*, May 20, 1987, p. 2 in *FBIS-SOV*, May 21, 1987, p. E7.

66. Moscow in Cambodian to Cambodia, March 8, 1988 in *FBIS-SOV*, March 9, 1988, p. 19; Moscow International Service in Vietnamese, April 12, 1988 in *FBIS-SOV*, April 13, 1988, p. 9; N. Ryzhkov speech, "Strengthening Mutual Understanding and Trust," *Pravda*, May 18, 1988, p. 4 in *FBIS-SOV*, May 18, 1988, p. 22; Gorbachev statement, Moscow TASS in English, May 18, 1988 in *FBIS-SOV*, May 19, 1988, pp. 17-18; and Moscow TASS in English, May 26, 1988 in *FBIS-SOV*, May 27, 1988, pp. 22-23.

67. *The Straits Times* (Singapore), May 3, 1988, p. 12 in *FBIS-SOV*, May 6, 1988, p. 22.

68. A. Golts, "Along the Path of a Settlement," *Krasnaya Zvezda*, May 31, 1988, p. 3 in *FBIS-SOV*, June 3, 1988, p. 35.

69. See, for example, Soviet Government Statement, Moscow TASS International Service, October 17, 1987 in *FBIS-SOV*, October 20, 1987, pp. 32-33; Moscow in Cambodian to Cambodia, April 30, 1988 in *FBIS-SOV*, May 3, 1988, p. 17; and Golts, "Along the Path of a Settlement," 34.

70. Moscow in Cambodian to Cambodia, June 8, 1988 in *FBIS-SOV*, June 10, 1988, p. 32. Hun Sen, however, went on to say: "Without outside assistance, the Pol Pot group cannot do anything. We insistently ask that all countries and people stop providing assistance to this group."

According to *Le Monde*, Soviet Deputy Foreign Minister Igor Rogachev "wants dialogue between Sihanouk and Hun Sen 'to continue,' and he has 'not lost hope of others joining them' — a reference to the other two factions of the Khmer resistance, namely Son Sann's front and the Khmers Rouges." *Le Monde*, April 28, 1988, p. 3 in *FBIS-SOV*, April 28, 1988, p. 6.

71. The official Soviet government statement of May 29, 1988, called for "a political settlement of the situation surrounding Cambodia in the spirit of national reconciliation, on the basis of recognition of the existing realities, and with the participation of all forces that are involved in the conflict in one way or another." This statement certainly does not exclude the Khmer Rouge. Moscow TASS International Service in Russian, May 29, 1988 in *FBIS-SOV*, May 31, 1988, pp. 25–26.

72. ACDA, *World Military Expenditures and Arms Transfers: 1987*, pp. 90, 127, and speeches of Robert Gates, October 1988.

73. According to Kurt Campbell, the MPLA's July 1987 offensive against UNITA was directed by Soviet General Konstantin Shaganovitch with the assistance of General Mikhail Petrov. Kurt M. Campbell, "Southern Africa in Soviet Foreign Policy," *Adelphi Papers*, no. 227 (Winter 1987/88), 9–10. See also William Claiborne, "Cuban, Soviet Advisers Key to Angolan Regime," *The Washington Post*, July 9, 1987.

74. David B. Ottaway, "Cuba Said to Boost Troop Strength in Angola," *Washington Post*, May 13, 1988.

75. On the Angola-Namibia settlement, see "Text of Pacts on Namibia Independence and a Pullout by Cuba," *New York Times*, December 23, 1988; and David B. Ottaway, "Angola, S. Africa, Cuba Sign Pacts on Namibia, Troop Pullout," *Washington Post*, December 23, 1988.

76. Moscow World Service in English, April 1, 1988 in *FBIS-SOV*, April 4, 1988, p. 24; and Moscow in Portuguese to Africa, April 1, 1988 in *FBIS-SOV*, April 4, 1988, p. 24.

77. Radio Moscow in Portuguese quoted the Angolan ambassador to Moscow as saying that "in our country there is no policy of national reconciliation as they have abroad." In addition, he said that UNITA leader Jonas Savimbi could also return to Luanda, but he would have to "answer for his crimes." Moscow in Portuguese to Africa, May 22, 1988 in *FBIS-SOV*, May 25, 1988, p. 42.

78. ACDA, *World Military Expenditures and Arms Transfers: 1987*, pp. 100, 127. Several U.S. government officials have told me that Soviet arms transfers to Ethiopia substantially increased in 1987.

79. Aleksandr Serbin, "Sensible Step," *Pravda*, April 9, 1988, p. 5 in *FBIS-SOV*, April 20, 1988, p. 38; Moscow TASS in English, April 26, 1988, and Moscow Domestic Service in Russian, April 26, 1988, both in *FBIS-SOV*, April 27, 1988, p. 27.

80. I. Tarutin, "In the North of Ethiopia," *Pravda*, January 31, 1988, p. 4 in *FBIS-SOV*, February 10, 1988, p. 37; idem, "'Former' People Take Up Arms," *Pravda*, March 20, 1988, p. 1 in *FBIS-SOV*, March 22, 1988, p. 37; Capt. 2nd Rank V. Kocherov, "Eritrea and Tigre Once Again," *Krasnaya Zvezda*, April 14, 1988, p. 3 in *FBIS-SOV*, April 21, 1988, pp. 21–22; I. Tarutin, "Eritrea Is a Stranger to Peace," *Pravda*, May 30, 1988, p. 6 in *FBIS-SOV*, June 3, 1988, p. 49; and Andrey Balebanov, "Splitists and Their Patrons," *Selskaya Zhizn*, June 9, 1988, p. 3 in *FBIS-SOV*, June 20, 1988, pp. 30–31.

81. Moscow TASS in English, May 6, 1988 in *FBIS-SOV*, May 9, 1988, p. 32 (emphasis added).

82. ACDA, *World Military Expenditures and Arms Transfers: 1987*, pp. 113, 129. According to Robert Gates, the Soviets and Cubans together gave Nicaragua nearly $1 billion in economic and military assistance in 1987.

83. A. Bovin, "Nicaragua in Struggle," *Izvestiya*, January 26, 1986, p. 5 in *FBIS-SOV*, January 30, 1986, p. K6.

84. *Krasnaya Zvezda* published an interesting justification for why the Duarte government should negotiate with the FMLN, but the Sandinistas should not have to negotiate with the contras: "Washington is making demands on Nicaragua that are incompatible with its sovereignty. It is stated in the form of an ultimatum, for example, that the Sandinists should start direct talks with the contras. The Salvadoran Government's talks with the representatives of the patriotic forces are cited as a model. But this is an obvious cheat! There is no civil war in Nicaragua. The country, it is stressed in Managua, is the object of aggression on the part of the United States; the contras are Washington's mercenaries and do not represent anyone. But in El Salvador, the revolutionary fronts are waging a war against an antipopular regime." M. Ponomarev, "Central America: Light at the End of the Tunnel?" *Kras-*

naya Zvezda, November 1, 1987, p. 3 in *FBIS-SOV*, November 12, 1987, p. 33.

85. In its reporting on the meetings, TASS stated: "Note was taken, among positive trends in settling conflict situations, of a desire for national reconciliation, the involvement of regional organizations, and the increased role of the United Nations. Shevardnadze stressed that the Soviet Union invariably follows a policy of principle directed at easing tension in Central America and achieving an early end to the undeclared war against Nicaragua. He expressed the firm conviction that the only possibility to ensure this is in a peaceful settlement of the regional conflict, just as of the other similar situations, by political means in the spirit of realism and with regard for the rightful interests of the sides concerned." Moscow TASS in English, February 26, 1988 in *FBIS-SOV*, February 26, 1988, p. 38.

86. "Against Interference," *Pravda*, May 3, 1988, p. 5 in *FBIS-SOV*, May 6, 1988, p. 33. For similar statements, see Moscow TASS in English, May 24, 1988 in *FBIS-SOV*, May 25, 1988, p. 49; and Moscow TASS in English, June 6, 1988 in *FBIS-SOV*, June 6, 1988, p. 52.

87. See Gorbachev's letter to Costa Rican President Arias in *La Republica* (San Jose), April 10, 1988, p. 4 in *FBIS-SOV*, April 20, 1988, p. 49. See also Shevardnadze press conference, Moscow TASS International Service in Russian, May 12, 1988 in *FBIS-SOV*, May 13, 1988, p. 9.

88. ACDA, *World Military Expenditures and Arms Transfers: 1987*, pp. 112, 127.

89. Moscow TASS in English, October 11, 1985 in *FBIS-SOV*, October 22, 1985, p. J3.

90. "Studio-74" interview with Atanasio [sic] Dimas, editor of the Mozambican paper *Domingo*, Moscow in Portuguese to Africa, May 17, 1988 in *FBIS-SOV*, May 24, 1988, p. 42.

91. "Pretoria in Pact with Mozambique," *New York Times*, May 26, 1988.

92. U.S. Department of Defense, *Soviet Military Power: 1987* (Washington, D.C., March 1987), 140–141, and talks with U.S. government officials.

93. ACDA, *World Military Expenditures and Arms Transfers: 1987*, pp. 124, 130.

94. Peter Grier, "Soviets Bolster an Arab Ally," *Christian Science Monitor*, March 11, 1988, and Avigdor Haselkorn, "Soviet

Détente Excludes Yemen," *The World & I* 3, no. 7 (July 1988): 101–105.

95. L. Val'kova, "Revolyutsiya krepnet v borb'e," *Aziya i Afrika Segodniya* (March 1988), 16–17.

96. Michael R. Gordon, "Soviets Scale Back Naval Deployments and Large Exercises," *New York Times*, July 17, 1988.

97. Mark N. Katz, "The Soviet-Cuban Connection," *International Security* 8, no. 1 (Summer 1983): 96.

98. The Soviets have broadcast this message to the Third World continuously since Gorbachev came to power. For more on this subject, see U.S. Department of State, *Soviet Influence Activities: A Report on Active Measures and Propaganda, 1986-87* (Washington, D.C.: Department of State, August 1987), chaps. 7–9.

99. One of the most prominent themes in Soviet propaganda under Gorbachev is U.S. "neoglobalism" or "new globalism." In discussing neoglobalism, or the "Reagan Doctrine," Moscow usually refers to U.S. assistance to guerrilla groups fighting Marxist regimes in Afghanistan, Nicaragua, Angola, Kampuchea, and sometimes Mozambique. The Soviets insist, however, that U.S. neoglobalism is directed toward the Third World as a whole. The United States does not just single out Marxist regimes, but pursues this policy against all governments that follow an "independent" foreign policy not liked by Washington. The Soviets portray Marxist regimes as being normal governments like any other in the Third World; because the United States fosters "aggression" against them, it could do so against any government.

Other examples of the neoglobalist policy include U.S. actions against Libya, the Levant, and in the Persian Gulf. Moscow claimed that U.S. "aggression" against Libya was undertaken because Libya refused to accept the U.S.-Israeli plan for a Middle East peace settlement. In doing this, the Soviets sought not only to portray Libya as the blameless victim of aggression, but also to warn other Arab states that the United States could do the same thing to them for not supporting U.S. policy in the Middle East.

Moscow claims that the concept of neoglobalism is nothing but the Reagan administration's justification for sponsoring terrorism and seeking to dominate the Third World. Moscow characterizes as terrorism such actions as the U.S. raids on Libya and the mining of Nicaraguan harbors. The targets of these hostile

U.S. actions are completely blameless and did nothing whatsoever to provoke this behavior.

Terrorism is a regular policy pursued by the U.S. government; Soviet propaganda terms it "state terrorism." As proof that the United States supports state terrorism, the Soviets point out that the United States did not vote for the Soviet-sponsored UN resolution condemning state terrorism.

The Soviets claim that U.S. state terrorism is evident not only in the above-mentioned instances, but also in support to anti-Soviet rebels in Afghanistan and other countries, the formation of the Rapid Deployment Force, supposed efforts to destabilize a number of Third World countries (especially India), and various assassination attempts. Soviet media have blamed the United States for the deaths of Patrice Lumumba, Salvador Allende, Omar Torrijos, Maurice Bishop, Orlando Letelier, Indira Gandhi, Mujibur Rahman, Zulfiqar Ali Bhutto, and other Third World leaders. Moscow has accused Washington of attempting to kill Rajiv Gandhi, among others.

100. Stephen Sestanovich, "Gorbachev's Foreign Policy: A Diplomacy of Decline," *Problems of Communism* 37, no. 1 (January–February 1988): 13.

101. Some analysts have cited the 1966 Tashkent agreement in which the Soviets successfully mediated a conclusion to the 1965 Indo-Pakistani war as a success for Moscow. See, for example, Robert Neumann, "Moscow's New Role as Mideast Broker," *Washington Post* (Outlook), October 25, 1987. In fact, its success was short-lived. The Soviet aim was to enhance Moscow's influence in both India (which was already its ally) and Pakistan (which had been allied to the West). But although the Soviets mediated an end to the conflict, they were unable to maintain influence with both. When the USSR attempted to enhance its position in Pakistan by selling arms to Islamabad, India objected strongly. Yet even though it received Soviet arms, Islamabad continued to ally with China. When Moscow later sided with India's intervention to defeat Pakistani forces in Bangladesh, it lost influence in Pakistan, which turned even closer to the West and China. The Soviets ended up right where they started – with some but certainly not predominant influence in India and no influence in Pakistan. See Charles B. McLane, *Soviet-Asian Relations* (London: Central Asian Research Centre, 1973), 56–57, 116–117.

The Soviet effort to mediate the growing conflict between

Ethiopia and Somalia in 1977 also ended with the Soviets' having influence in one country but not the other. Only on this occasion, Moscow gained a new ally (Ethiopia) but lost an old one (Somalia). See Bruce D. Porter, *The USSR in Third World Conflicts* (Cambridge: Cambridge University Press, 1984), 194–196.

102. Moscow TV Service in Russian, July 28, 1986 in *FBIS-SOV*, July 29, 1986, pp. R16–18.

103. Paul Wolfowitz, "Southeast Asia – Deferring Hard Choices," *The National Interest*, no. 12 (Summer 1988): 126.

104. Philip Taubman, "Gorbachev Offers Disputed Radar for Peaceful Exploration of Space," *New York Times*, September 17, 1988.

105. See, for example, Moscow World Service in English, August 28, 1987 in *FBIS-SOV*, August 28, 1987, p. 11; Leonid Kuznetsov, "The Fifth Putsch," *New Times*, no. 37 (September 21, 1987), 12–14; and Moscow TASS in English, October 26, 1987 in *FBIS-SOV*, October 29, 1987, p. 33.

106. Philip C. Boobbyer, "Soviet Perceptions of the South Pacific in the 1980s," *Asian Survey* 28, no. 5 (May 1988): 577–579.

107. Ibid., 583–585.

108. Wolfowitz, "Southeast Asia – Deferring Hard Choices," 122.

109. ACDA, *World Military Expenditures and Arms Transfers: 1987*, pp. 105, 129.

110. Richard W. Murphy, "The Persian Gulf: Stakes and Risks," *Current Policy*, no. 963 (U.S. Department of State, June 1987): 2–3.

111. Don Oberdorfer, "Soviet Deal with Kuwait Spurred U.S. Ship Role," *Washington Post*, May 24, 1987.

112. See, for example, Moscow TASS in English, June 24, 1987 in *FBIS-SOV*, June 25, 1987, pp. E1–2.

113. Flora Lewis, "Soviet Aide Says Navy Won't Add Warships in Gulf," *New York Times*, June 7, 1987.

114. Philip Taubman, "Iran and Soviet Draft Big Projects, Including Pipelines and Railroad," *New York Times*, August 15, 1987.

115. David Shipler, "Soviet Links Iran Embargo to UN Force," *New York Times*, December 17, 1987.

116. A. Bovin, "Frontline Kuwait," *Izvestiya*, May 11, 1988, p. 5 in *FBIS-SOV*, May 13, 1988, p. 16. Bovin noted that the Kuwaitis were grateful not only to Soviet sailors for their "hard

and dangerous work," but to sailors from the United States and other countries as well.

117. For an excellent analysis of Soviet policy toward the Middle East since Gorbachev came to power, see Galia Golan, "Gorbachev's Middle East Strategy," *Foreign Affairs* 66, no. 1 (Fall 1987): 41–57. See also "Meet Mikhail Gorbachev's Pariah Diplomacy," 39–40.

118. See, for example, ibid., 49–50, and Alexei Makovsky, "Strings Attached," *New Times*, no. 41 (October 19, 1987): 8.

119. Robert Pear, "U.S. Says Soviets Are Expanding Base for Warships on Syrian Coast," *New York Times*, August 28, 1988.

120. David E. Albright, *Soviet Policy toward Africa Revisited* (Washington, D.C.: Center for Strategic and International Studies, 1987), 140; Lisa Anderson, "Libya's Qaddafi: Still in Command?" *Current History* 86 (February 1987): 67–68, 86–87; and International Institute for Strategic Studies, *Strategic Survey, 1987-1988* (London, 1988), 187–188.

121. "Crumbling North," *The Economist*, June 4, 1988, p. 40. According to U.S. and North Yemeni government officials I spoke with, Moscow played an important role in arranging a peaceful settlement to a border dispute between North and South Yemen in the spring of 1988.

122. Fukuyama, "Patterns of Soviet Third World Policy," 8, and Prizel, "Latin America: The Long March," 109–120.

Index